Praise fc

"The description of Sharon's journey shows us not only her physical healing, it also shares her spiritual transformation. The "gut level" honesty filled me with compassion, admiration and reverence. Although her experience will be valuable to those learning about concussions, Sharon's combination of determination and vulnerability show us who she is. Readers will be inspired and informed. We each have our own sacred story. This record of her journey shows us that Sharon is no longer just a flash but an enduring light of wisdom."

—Rita Otis, Tai Chi Instructor
and Spiritual Leader

"Sharon Royers does an amazing job illustrating what professionals rattle off as the 'check list' of concussion symptoms in her personal story, *Out of the Rabbit Hole*. The check list never does justice to the true reality of concussion. The way in which Sharon shares what works, what doesn't, and the reality of accepting and adapting along the way is very powerful. I loved this book and would encourage anyone wanting to gain a glimpse into the reality of concussion recovery to read, *Out of the Rabbit Hole*.

—Peggy Reisher, Executive Director
Brain Injury Alliance of Nebraska

"*Out of the Rabbit Hole* is an inspiration. Many of Sharon's experiences and struggles with recovery resonated with my own recovery process. I, too, tried to do more than I should have at first and was frustrated with not accomplishing goals I had set. Sharon's accident was like anyone's who has suffered any kind of traumatic brain injury. Some injuries can be classified as mild and some severe but both are life changing. It takes time for everyone who is injured to accept, understand and overcome any issues they might experience in their lifetime after the traumatic accident. I like to say that Hope and Glory never leaves anyone, they are always there for you. This book is truly a light of Hope for the brain injured community!"

—Micah J. Fulmer, Brain Injury Survivor

"I am grateful for *Out of the Rabbit Hole*. It is well written and easy to read for a difficult and complex subject. I came to see concussion in an entirely different light than what I had known before reading this book, thank you!"

—Rev. Dr. Don Sarton,
Parent of a Brain Injury Survivor

Out of the Rabbit Hole

How a Concussion Changed My Life: A Story of Hope

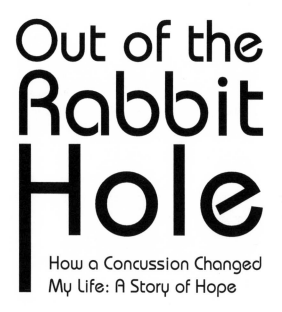

Sharon Royers, M.S., M.A.

HOPE

Omaha, Nebraska

OUT OF THE RABBIT HOLE: HOW A CONCUSSION CHANGED MY LIFE: A STORY OF HOPE

For inquiries contact:
sroyers26@gmail.com
www.HopeForConcussion.com

Paperback ISBN: 978-1-7321046-0-0
Mobi ISBN: 978-1-7321046-1-7
EPUB ISBN: 978-1-7321046-2-4

Printed in the USA

10 9 8 7 6 5 4 3 2

This book is dedicated to my family.

Their love and support was invaluable
as I meandered my way through
the healing process.

Contents

Foreword

Although *Out of the Rabbit Hole* is written from a personal experience it rings true as a mythic tale about loss, recovery, triumph. Story has the power to transcend personal experience; to connect us to a universal consciousness. There are questions we all ask and must answer on our spiritual journey: Who am I if I am not who I thought I was? Is it really okay to not do anything? We all have dragons we must slay. We all have symbols of hope that come when needed. It is interesting that Sharon, the Flash, a brilliant but temporary light, needed sustained darkness to heal; like the hero on his journey who descends to the depths and must learn a new way of seeing using unrecognized gifts. Sharon's story clearly shows the body has a wisdom that can be used to navigate this journey. Our body is our friend, ever present companion, guide and teacher. The problem is that what it whispers often does not seem true to who we think we should be. We do not listen until we are forced to take the journey.

While reading *Out of the Rabbit Hole*, I found the story resonated deeply with many layers of my own journey. As a Tai Chi Chih/Qi Gong teacher and Body Wisdom Interplay leader, this story spoke to my search for metaphysical truth. I remembered seeing a movie sometime in the 70's that showed people trying to reach "enlightenment" by hitting themselves in the head with a large white soft ball. As her book attests, a bonk on the head is not the easy way to learn about consciousness and enlightenment. It seems to me that the practices Sharon used to cope and rest are similar to the spiritual practices used by Christian Mystics, Buddhist meditators and Chinese Qi Gong healers to let Divine Mystery make truth known to the human mind. These spiritual practices take us on a unique inward journey that is transformational but, like a bonk on the head, may not always be pleasant. No matter what causes us to begin the spiritual journey, we need guides along the way. *Out of the Rabbit Hole* is a worthy guidebook.

—Rita Otis, Tai Chi Chih/Qi Gong Teacher and Spiritual Leader

Acknowledgments

There have been so many people who came into my life just at the right time to help me along my healing journey, as well as support me with writing this book. I would like to first thank Janet Tilden, my editor. I would also like to thank Rachel Moore, cover designer, web site designer, and hand-holder through the self-publishing process.

I am grateful for my family physician, specialists, physical, occupational, and speech therapists. I am so fortunate to live in Omaha—a community with such high-quality health care.

I would like to thank the staff and students of Indian Hill Elementary School for their love and support. Their understanding and encouragement meant the world to me.

A special thank you goes to my dear friend, Susan Mayberger, who offered encouragement as I wrestled with the writing process. She was a sounding board, cheerleader, and faithful friend.

My heart is also filled with much gratitude for the numerous instructors and trainers who came into my life at just the right time. Thank you to Rita Otis who shared her peace and joy through the Tai Chi Chih classes she taught. Thank you to the staff at the Armbrust Acres YMCA who were always so patient and understanding: Jill Grindstaff, Trainer; John Hurt, Tai Chi instructor; and Anita Whittle, Yoga instructor. I am also so grateful for the people at LoveYourBrain Yoga and Carole Westerman at Evolve To Harmony Yoga Studio. And a special note of gratitude to Maureen Feeney of River Point Acupuncture. Her expertise in the healing art of acupuncture as well as her wry sense of humor were invaluable to my healing process.

I am grateful for Peggy Reisher, the Brain Injury Alliance of Nebraska, and the many brain injury survivors I have met who both humble and inspire me.

And finally, the unwavering love and support of my children, family, and friends was the life line I clung to when hope felt far away. I cannot name them all here, but I must express my deepest love and gratitude to my dear husband, Rick Royers. He is my rock and I could not have survived the concussion recovery journey without him. Also, I give a big hug and thank you to my best friend and sister, Deb Clouthier. Rick and Deb are my calm when the seas are stormy. I am so blessed to have you two in my life.

Introduction

The yellowing varnish revealed its age. Its hinges worked just fine. They did not squeak as old cabinet doors often do. But the latch was another matter. On the surface, the cabinet door appeared to be in working order. Just like me. But after my concussion, very little about me was still in working order.

I grappled with whether to write this book. It was challenging both emotionally and cognitively to describe the years when I was caught in the web of post-concussion syndrome (PCS). I also wrestled with how to label my experience. When I searched for a definition, I found that a *rabbit hole* is "a bizarre, confusing, or nonsensical situation or environment, typically one from which it is difficult to extricate oneself." This is a perfect description of my life after hitting my head on an old cabinet door.

According to the U.S. Centers for Disease Control and Prevention, 1.7 million people sustain a traumatic brain injury each year.

Although concussion is classified as a mild traumatic brain injury, it is often very debilitating for injured persons and their loved ones. With proper care, most people with concussions return to full health after a week or two. However, about 30 percent of concussion patients still have symptoms up to three months later. And about 15 percent of patients continue to have symptoms after a year or more.

One of the reasons I felt compelled to write this book is that I believe PCS is a significant female health issue that has not received enough attention. I certainly had not heard of it before my head injury. There is an abundance of information about concussions, but most of this information involves male athletes or athletes in general. Yet research indicates that females suffer more concussions than males, have more severe symptoms, and often need more time to recover. Just as women's cardiac symptoms and treatment needs differ from those of men, so do our symptoms and treatment needs after concussions. Females are much more vulnerable than men to being caught in the web of PCS. I believe that if men were more vulnerable to this condition, *post-concussion syndrome* would become a household term.

In her book *Wrestling with Angels*, Naomi Rosenblatt writes, "But how often do our best intentions seem to turn back on us like a bad dream. Why is it that we frequently start out to fix a problem, only to find we've created a worse one?" This is a story of my bad dream: my tumble down the rabbit hole of post-concussion syndrome (PCS) and my journey out. Chapters 1–12 describe the challenges and triumphs of my healing journey. Chapter 13 is a summary of resources and strategies that worked for me.

I share my story to offer hope to others who may be stuck in the darkness of the rabbit hole.

1

The Flash

The paradox of post-concussion syndrome is that you desperately miss your former life: the person you were before the head injury. But the more you want your life back and the more you reach for it, the farther down the rabbit hole you fall. You find yourself in a dark place where life is happening all around you, but you can't quite connect with it. You long to be able to do all the things you used to do: drive a car with the radio on, shop without being bothered by the lights and sounds, get up at 5:30 in the morning and go for a two-mile jog, kayak off the coast of Maine with your husband, race your granddaughter down the slide.

During the summer prior to my concussion I was in the best physical shape of my life. I had been running a few miles several times a week for decades. It was my cheap way of staying in shape, as well as a way to carve out time alone as a busy mom and educator. Most importantly, running was a highly effective way to relieve stress. I wasn't a marathon runner and had never wanted to be. My bad knees wouldn't have allowed it, but they tolerated a moderate two- to three-mile jog quite nicely. After decades of running, however, I noticed that my 50-something body was losing ground and I knew it was time to change my exercise routine a bit. I began riding my bike more often as well as increasing my sit-ups and push-ups. The summer prior to my concussion I was running four to five times a week and riding my bike 10 to 20 miles three times a week with ease. I was crunching out 60 sit-ups and 40 push-ups five times a week. My body was firming up, and I felt great!

I've never been a fan of heat and humidity, so each summer my husband Rick and I made a trip to the coast of Maine to escape the sultry Nebraska weather. The summer before I hit my head, we made our annual trek out east as usual, with both of my sisters joining us. It was a time to relax with family and get energized before the next school year began. We enjoyed exploring the coast, visiting our mother's childhood stomping grounds, and relaxing together. Rick and I kayaked in the Atlantic. My sister joined us on a hike up Mount Battie, and my husband and sister had a difficult time keeping up with me. They would become breathless as we climbed, but I was energized and barely breaking a sweat. I was in the best shape I had been in since childhood. I loved being physically active. It was a core part of who I was.

August came quickly and another school year was underway. I was in my sixth year as principal of Indian Hill Elementary School in Omaha, Nebraska. The school had been labeled "failing" when I came on board, and my mission was to turn it around. Indian Hill served an ethnically diverse, high-poverty student population of about 600 students from kindergarten through sixth grade. We not only served the largest government housing project in the state, but we also had a high percentage of English Language Learners (ELLs). Our ELLs were a mix of migrants, immigrants, and refugees. This was not your typical "kiss a pig when the kids meet their reading goals" elementary school principalship. My job was demanding, and I took my role very seriously. I was well aware that the only ticket out of poverty for my Indian Hill students was a high-quality education. No small order.

The school's head custodian enjoyed doling out nicknames to the staff. One teacher who was always well-dressed received the moniker "Hollywood." Another teacher had a strong southern drawl, so he called her "Mississippi." I was known for speeding around the building in my suits and running shoes, so I was dubbed "Flash." I embraced this nickname. Every principal wants to be cool, and I thought being Flash made me kind of cool. My own children even gave me a Flash T-shirt for Mother's Day. I was THE Flash.

I ran regularly to cope with the stress of my job. I often awoke at 5:30, put on the running clothes that I had laid out the night before, laced up my Asics and drove to the nearby high school track. The surface of the track was gentler on my aging knees than pavement would have been. Also, the track was near the base of a hill, so it was away from street lights. Looking up at the clear, starry sky during my early morning runs was both meditative and energizing. These early-morning runs helped me stay on my game during the long, stressful school days.

Just weeks before I hit my head, I was sitting at a conference table with my leadership team making plans for the new school year. Our first five years of implementing our school improvement plan had worked so well that we had become the model for all the other Title I schools in the district. Our instructional coaches were very talented and instrumental in our school's improvement process. One of my roles was to help them continue to hone their leadership skills, so we had decided to create and share personal leadership goals for the new school year. I shared, unnecessarily, that I tended to do things too quickly—think, talk, walk, even listen. My staff looked at me with knowing eyes, as if my revelation was no surprise to them. After all, I was the Flash. I confessed to my team of leaders that I realized buzzing about the building at full throttle all the time wasn't necessarily a good thing. My goal for the new school year was to slow down. Be more mindful. Walk and talk a little more slowly, listen more deeply. I think my exact words were that I wanted to "learn to be still." I would soon discover that the Universe has a wicked sense of humor.

2

The Cabinet Door

The morning of September 24, 2014 is etched in my mind. I had been looking for a file on a new sixth-grade student. He had been very respectful and polite during the first few weeks of school—almost overly so. So I was surprised and a little disturbed when I returned to the building one day after an administrators' meeting to find my assistant principal looking a bit frazzled. She reported that there had been an incident with our new sixth-grade student. He had punched a girl in the back of the head during class. When the assistant principal questioned him about what happened, he'd had a complete meltdown. He screamed at her, called her a racist, and then ran from her office after she told him that he would be placed on in-school suspension. These behaviors seemed out of character for the polite student I had observed earlier.

I felt that I had established a positive rapport with this young man, so I purposely stationed myself outside the cafeteria door before breakfast the next morning so I could greet him and talk with him about what had happened the day before. As he approached the door, I put my arm around his shoulder and took him aside, not wanting to embarrass him in front of the other students. I expressed my shock about what had happened and asked him what was going on. He immediately became very emotional and shouted, "You're *all* racists!" He turned and ran in the direction of the housing project where he lived.

I quickly went inside to call his parents. As I was leaving messages, I watched through my office window as he reentered the school. He was with a tall, older woman I assumed to be his grandmother. She was wearing her work uniform and looked to be in her fifties or sixties. It was hard to tell how old she actually was, but she looked like she had lived a hard life.

The three of us sat at the round table in my office and began discussing what was happening with this young man. His grandmother listened patiently, and when I had finished explaining the out-of-character behavior he had displayed, she asked him to wait outside my office. With the office door closed, she privately summarized for me her grandson's story. He had been given to her at birth because he had crack in his system. Her daughter had severe drug addiction issues, so this grandmother was now raising all three of her sons. She also explained that all three boys had been sexually abused when they were very young. This background information helped to explain the explosive emotions we were now seeing.

Indian Hill Elementary, with its 95 percent poverty rate, was not without resources. Omaha is a community blessed with caring philanthropists and visionaries. Our school was one of the first to get a full-time mental health therapist who served our children in the school, during the school day. I explained the therapy services as an option to the grandmother. She looked as though a weight had been lifted off her shoulders, and she did not hesitate to request services for her grandson. As I left her with the therapist to discuss the details of her grandson's story, she appeared less defeated and a little more hopeful.

The information I had just received certainly helped explain my new student's behaviors, but I felt that I didn't have the full picture yet. I wanted to be able to support him, so I felt compelled to read his cumulative folder. This is a file that is kept on each student throughout the elementary years. By reading this student's file, I would be able to see how many times he had changed schools, review his academic data, and most importantly, read his past teachers' comments about his social-emotional development.

During the school year, the cumulative folders were stored in the classrooms for easy access by the teachers. I went to the student's homeroom to get the file. His teacher was absent that day, so a substitute was leading the lesson. (If his teacher had been present, I simply would have emailed and asked her to bring me his file.) I tiptoed along the wall nearest the door in an attempt to avoid interrupting instruction. I spotted a file cabinet in the back of the room and thought it might be a logical place to find the file.

The classroom had a wall of built-in cabinets that had been installed when the building was constructed in 1957. I had to tiptoe past these cabinets to access the file drawers. I noticed that the last cabinet door was ajar and a few sheets of construction paper were peeking out. I quietly put the paper back in the cabinet and pushed the door closed. I then began shuffling through the file drawers, looking for the student's cumulative folder. I started with the top drawer and worked my way down. As I knelt down to search through the bottom drawer, I remember hearing the crack of my knees popping and feeling the pain of kneeling on the hard floor.

I did not find the file I was looking for, so I stood up quickly, ready to scurry off to my next task. I didn't notice that the cabinet door had once again popped open. I stood straight up into it and hit the upper right side of my head hard. I must have said something, because the whole class turned toward me. Several students asked if I was okay. Feeling embarrassed that I had interrupted the lesson, I assured everyone that I was fine and quickly left the classroom.

Once I was in the hallway I stopped to touch my head to see if I was bleeding. I felt a painful tingling sensation and was sure I had injured my scalp and would need stitches. I touched the top of my head and then looked at my hand expecting to see blood. But there was no blood. I began walking toward my office and stopped again. I remember feeling very strange, almost loopy. The caricature of the cartoon character who hits his head and starts seeing stars swirling about comes to mind. It was like that—I just didn't feel right.

I continued into my office, slipping past the secretaries. For some reason I felt embarrassed and did not want anyone to know I had hit my head. After all, super heroes like The Flash are invincible; they don't get hurt. I decided to shake off the incident and get back to work. I sat down in my office chair and began to do something, but I couldn't remember what I wanted to do. After several attempts to do something on my computer and drawing a complete blank, I decided to ask the school nurse to check the pupils of my eyes. The possibility of a concussion crossed my mind, but I mistakenly believed that the pupils will dilate unevenly if someone has a concussion.

Again, I was careful not to let my staff in the office know I had hit my head. The nurse had her own office adjacent to the room where she treated sick or injured students. I stepped into her office and closed the door behind me. I told her that I had hit my head standing up into a cabinet door and a lump was forming on the upper right side of my head. I mentioned that it was becoming painful to open my mouth to speak because the lump was at the top of the muscle that moves the jaw. I told the nurse that I felt like I'd had my bell rung. I explained that I was quite confused and kept forgetting what I was doing, and I asked her to check my pupils. She examined my pupils and said they were dilating normally. She suggested that I take a few Advil and assured me that I would be fine.

I returned to my office thinking that I was making a big deal out of a simple bump on the head. Little did I know that there was nothing simple about it.

The events of that evening at home are mostly a blur to me. The only real memory I have of that evening was that it hurt to eat dinner. Chewing, talking, or doing anything that engaged my jaw muscle sent sharp pains through the now-sizable lump on my head. I don't specifically remember a headache, however.

Still under the false impression that I had simply bumped my head, I got up at 5:30 the next morning and drove to the nearby high school track for my morning run. The sky was still dark, and it was a clear, crisp fall morning. I don't remember having a headache when I began running. I might have had one, but if it was not severe I would have run anyway. But by the time I had completed two miles my head was throbbing so much that it seemed ready to split open. I somehow managed to shower and drive myself to school—a 30-minute commute. I have no memory of arriving at school. I do remember sitting down at my desk and feeling like I had been hit by a Mack truck. In addition to severe fatigue, I experienced a sense of intense pressure and squeezing, almost as if an elephant had decided to sit on my head.

At that moment I knew I'd had a concussion, so I opened my web browser and did an Internet search on the word "concussion." I checked off the basic symptoms: headache, confusion, pressure. Yep, I had a concussion. The web site recommended being still and resting. It was Thursday morning, so there were just two school days left until the weekend. I remember thinking I could muddle through two more days and then rest over the weekend. After all, the school district doesn't send substitutes for principals. We were only a month into the new school year and I felt that I needed to be present to make sure the ship continued pointing in the right direction.

By the time Friday afternoon rolled around, I was miserable. As soon as I got home, I curled up on the couch in the fetal position and informed my son and husband that I would not be moving a muscle all weekend because I needed to rest my head. Getting up only to eat and go to the bathroom, I spent the entire weekend sleeping.

I felt remarkably better by Monday morning and went to school as usual. My head pain and pressure were gone and I remember feeling symptom-free. My husband made me promise to call our doctor if I started to feel sick again, so I told him I would. About an hour into the school day as I was responding to emails, problem solving with teachers, and whirling-twirling around in my usual Flash style, the elephant landed on my head again with a vengeance.

I'm not sure why I was so hesitant to see my doctor. Denial was probably the primary factor. It was a very inconvenient time to be out of commission. I was so busy getting the new school year off the ground that I simply did not have time for a concussion. But by that afternoon my brain fog had rolled back in and I could no longer think straight. I picked up the phone and called my family physician's office. She had time to see me on Wednesday, exactly one week after I had hit my head.

I continued working that Tuesday. The pain and fog seemed to ebb and flow with my stress levels. I have very little memory of that day and am pretty sure I just soldiered through it. What else could I do?

My appointment was on Wednesday morning, immediately after the doctor's office opened. I woke up feeling better; sleep seemed to help enormously. I felt so much better that I almost canceled the appointment. When my doctor walked into the examining room I summarized for her what had happened and described my symptoms. I mentioned feeling confused and showed her the lump that was still on my head a week later. It was still a little painful to open my jaw. I expressed to her that I was pretty sure I'd had a concussion, but I was over it and only visiting with her because I had promised my husband I would. I did not want to have a concussion, so I was working hard to will it away.

Throughout my life, this gritty toughness of pushing through the pain was my mode of operation. In high school, the principal called me "Grin"—short for "Grin and bear it." (My maiden name was Barrett, so the nickname was a play on my last name as well as my personality.) Every strength we have is also a weakness. I was soon going to learn that there is a time to push through and a time to surrender and be still.

My doctor assured me that she was certified in concussion care and had even served on a committee for developing concussion care protocols. Woohoo—score! I had always loved my family doctor; she had taken care of all my children, grandchildren, and even my father before he passed away. So she knew me and my whole family very well. She is a patient, thorough, and caring doctor. For her to have special training in concussion care was a bonus.

Although I had assured her I was fine, she examined me anyway. She asked me the standard dementia questions: *What is today's date? Who is the president of the United States? Spell "world" backwards. Count backwards from 100 by 7's*. Just a year earlier I had sat in her office listening to her pose the same questions to my elderly father. We had both passed the test. Next she had me stand on one foot with my eyes closed so she could check my balance. She had me walk heel-to-toe across the exam room. She checked my eyes for tracking. I don't remember how I did; I just remember her suggesting that I take the ImPACT test.

The ImPACT test is a computer program designed to get baseline data for athletes for purposes of comparison when they have head injuries to determine whether they have a concussion. First you enter personal information such as age and education level. Then ImPACT checks cognitive function by measuring memory and response time, among other things. I remember sitting at a desk and entering my personal information. Female. 54 years old. Two master's degrees. After I had answered all the personal questions, the directions for the test popped up. At this point, my brain was very tired. I had just passed the doctor's examination and entered information into the computer, and I needed a break. But I tried to push on. I kept reading the directions on the computer screen over and over again. I could read the words, but I could not comprehend them. It was as if my brain had become Teflon and word meanings were bouncing off rather than being absorbed. And this wasn't even the test yet! These were only the directions.

I decided to bypass the directions, hit Enter, and give the test my best shot. There was a list of items I was supposed to remember. Then the computer had me do some other simple tasks, and then I was asked to recall the items it had shown me previously. No can do! My memory, like my ability to comprehend written directions, was like Swiss cheese all of a sudden—full of holes. I simply couldn't perform the required tasks.

The results of the ImPACT test were available immediately. My doctor read them and smiled patiently at me. She announced that I indeed had a concussion and should take the rest of the week off. This was Wednesday morning, so including the weekend I would have a total of four and a half days of rest. "That should do it!" I thought.

My doctor's orders were to rest, limit TV and computer viewing, and eat light. I hadn't run in a week and I exercised both for stress relief and weight control. So when my doctor told me to eat light, I thought she was worried that I was going to gain weight. I would later find out why it's important to eat light after a concussion. My doctor said I could return to work on Monday if I felt up to it, but she wanted me to see her again first thing on Tuesday morning.

I followed the doctor's orders to the letter. I did not watch TV, limited my email check-ins, and mostly slept. I felt very tired, almost as if I had been drugged. Sleep felt like salve on a wound. It was wonderfully healing.

While I was still at home resting, my cell phone rang. It was my assistant principal, so I answered right away, thinking that there must have been an emergency at school. She was calling to let me know that she had just found out she needed foot surgery and was going to have it soon. I remember thinking this was not a problem, since I would be over my concussion by Sunday.

After complete rest for 4½ days I felt much better. My energy had returned, my head did not hurt, and I was thinking clearly. I returned to work that Monday and for the most part sailed through the day symptom-free. I saw my doctor the next morning and was still feeling well. During her exam she noted that my balance was much improved and my eye movements appeared normal. She had me take the ImPACT test again, and this time I passed with flying colors. I was able to read the directions and comprehend. The memory portions of the test were a challenge, but I was able to use mental strategies to pass the test. I was all better, and just in time, because I was needed back at school.

My doctor's final words of advice to me were to wait a week before returning to running. She also emphasized the importance of taking breaks at work. She said I should pace myself and continue taking it easy. It was at this point that I distinctly remember thinking, "Yeah, right! I'm an elementary school principal in a high-needs school. 'Take it easy' is NOT an option!" I didn't say those words aloud, of course; I simply smiled and nodded in response to the doctor's advice. At that point I had no clue how important it would be to follow her instructions, and I did not realize that concussions could get worse.

I returned to school full-time, and within the first week I was tumbling quickly down the rabbit hole. It was a dark, steep hole that I would soon discover is like a Chinese finger trap. The more you try to escape it, the more tightly entrapped you become.

Being the principal of Indian Hill Elementary was a rewarding but very taxing job. Some days were more taxing than others. I remember one particular day soon after my return to work. My assistant principal was out on medical leave for several weeks due to her foot surgery, so I was running the ship solo. As I entered the school office first thing that morning, I was told that in addition to the assistant principal being out of commission, one of the secretaries was running late and three teachers were out ill with no substitutes available. Normal me, pre-concussion me, could have handled all of this with ease. In fact, normal me enjoyed the challenge of multi-tasking and problem-solving. Like a knight slaying dragons, I relished taking down one problem at a time. But now my brain imploded with pain and immense pressure. The Flash's fast-thinking brain was not up to the task. I could not think clearly enough to solve the problems before me. My adrenaline kicked in and anxiety rose to flood levels. Strangely, I was not aware that my body's reaction to the stress had anything to do with the concussion. I just knew that somehow I had to make my brain function so I could do my job. The school secretary helped me to split the classrooms where there were no available teachers, and I somehow managed to muddle through the rest of the day with an elephant sitting on my head.

Fogginess and fatigue had rolled back in, and it took all my energy to make the 30-minute drive home that evening. I remember sitting on the couch to unwind with some mindless TV but I couldn't do it. I snapped at my husband to turn down the volume on the TV because I couldn't stand the noise. The lights suddenly seemed equally irritating. I remember the look on Rick's face after I snapped at him. He stared at me as if I had become someone else, a stranger. Neither of us realized that this stranger would be staying with us for a long while.

My symptoms of light and sound sensitivity, fogginess, and head pressure continued. Now I was free-falling at warp speed down the rabbit hole. How could I be getting worse after feeling better? None of it made sense to me as I returned once again to my family physician. The fluorescent lighting in the doctor's office was extremely irritating. The chatter and background noise in the office was overwhelming. It was as if I heard every sound all at once and could not focus on one at a time. My filter was broken and I just wanted to crawl into a dark, silent space to rest.

My doctor checked my eye movements by asking me to follow her finger with my eyes, as she had done during my previous visits. I was not tracking her finger normally this time; my eyeballs were jittery. She had me stand on one leg and close my eyes for a basic balance check. I could not do it. She asked me to walk heel-toe across the small exam room. I could not do it. It wasn't that I was dizzy, like many people with concussions. Instead, I was experiencing a sensation that I described as "warping." I felt as though I was walking on a ship that was being tossed about at sea. I could not get a grip on my balance. My symptoms had not been this severe when I had seen my doctor the first two times. How could my condition have become worse instead of better? I hadn't hit my head again. I could not comprehend what was going on with my body.

My doctor ordered me to stop working for the next four to six weeks. She prescribed physical therapy to help with my ocular motor and balance issues. She also prescribed medicine to help me sleep and relax so my brain could heal. The dark hole known as post-concussion syndrome had sucked me in, and it was not going to let go of me anytime soon.

3

Falling Down the Rabbit Hole

The next six weeks would be one of the most difficult periods in my life. My light sensitivity had become worse. Any light felt like sandpaper was being rubbed on my brain—it was simply intolerable. I now had to sleep with an eye mask on for complete darkness. I also used the mask to rest. I continued to be sound-sensitive as well. I was unable to watch TV. I checked in with my work emails once a day so they would not pile up, but otherwise I stayed away from my phone and computer screens.

I tried taking the 25 mg of Amitriptyline my doctor had prescribed. This medication is commonly used for concussions to help relax the injured brain so it can heal. I found that the medicine made me very sleepy, but also dizzy and very constipated—two side effects that are uncomfortable for anyone, but doubly so for a concussion patient. I stopped taking the medicine after a week. Without it, I struggled to fall asleep. There was a loud buzzing in my head that I could not quiet no matter what I tried. I would lie in bed with my eye mask on and just try to remain sane. Trying to quiet my injured brain so that I could sleep was one of the most difficult parts of the entire healing process. Once sleep finally came, I typically slept about 12 hours a night. I also napped most of the day. My doctor explained that all the sleeping was my brain's way of trying to heal, so I didn't fight it. I was unable to watch videos, listen to music, or read, so sleep was my only escape. It was like being trapped in solitary confinement in my own mind.

At this point driving a car was out of the question. My reaction time was much too slow, I couldn't think clearly enough to focus, and the light and sound sensitivity made it simply impossible. My husband became my chauffeur. Attempting to keep our sense of humor about the situation, Rick called it "Driving Miss Daisy" as he chauffeured me back and forth between doctor visits and physical therapy sessions. Rick had a demanding job at the headquarters of Union Pacific Railroad. Taking time off to drive me twice a week to physical therapy and follow-up doctor appointments was a strain on him. In addition, he had to run the household alone because all I could do was sleep, eat, and occasionally shower. And just sixteen days prior to my head injury, we had buried his father, Emil Jean Royers. Emil was 93 years old when he passed and had lived a long, happy life. Rick had been close to his father and although his death was expected, it was still difficult. Taking care of me was derailing Rick's natural grieving process and I felt guilty. My concussion was affecting my husband and my entire family. It was affecting my school. I was acutely aware of this and felt helpless to do anything about it.

Rick also felt helpless as he watched my symptoms worsen. He had a trusted friend from his karate dojo who also happened to be an emergency room doctor. Rick's friend was concerned that perhaps I had actually had a stroke or something worse than a concussion, considering the severity of my symptoms. He suggested that Rick bring me to the emergency room if I continued to get worse. On a Sunday morning in late October I woke up with continued light sensitivity, balance issues, and sound sensitivity. Out of frustration with what seemed to be a stalled healing process, Rick phoned his friend and we decided to trek to the emergency room for further investigation.

Once there, I was made comfortable in one of the exam rooms in the ER. They turned off the fluorescent lighting and I simply lay still while waiting for a series of doctors to come and go. They asked me the standard dementia questions again, just as my doctor had. They had me touch my nose with my fingers, track their pens with my eyes, and attempt to walk across the exam room heel-to-toe. It was decided that I should have a CT scan to rule out any bleeding.

Hours later I was wheeled to the area where CT scans are performed. I had to put my sweatshirt over my eyes because the fluorescent lighting in the hallway felt too bright and harsh. I was nervous about the scan. Not about the potential results, but just about surviving the process. By now it was late afternoon. I had not napped and was thirsty and hungry. It is normal to feel "off" under these conditions, but a concussed brain has very little tolerance for this. There is no wiggle room, no capacity to accommodate discomfort. Meanwhile, the invisible forceps was tightening its grip on my head and the pain was increasing.

The pain wasn't unbearable, but I was starting to panic. I resorted to using my breathing strategies from childbirth to get through the procedure. Another symptom of concussion is that the adrenal system gets out of whack, so the intense feeling of fight or flight sets in easily and very rapidly.

Being tired, hungry, and thirsty was compounding my body's reactions. I was able to breathe through the scan, however, and soon I was wheeled back to the exam room where my faithful husband waited with me in the dark.

The results of the CT scan were in. No bleeding. There was fluid in my mastoid, though, and now the doctor was concerned about my right ear. (The mastoid is a part of the skull behind the ear that contains open spaces.) I explained that the right side of my head had hit the cabinet, but my ear was not hurting at all. Because my symptoms did not include ear pain, the doctor dropped his concern about the mastoid and decided to refer me to a neurologist. This meant more waiting in the exam room. The neurologist finally arrived and examined me. I was asked the standard dementia questions again. I could spell "world" backwards. I knew that Barack Obama was the president of the United States. I knew what day of the week it was. Again, I was asked to walk and struggled greatly with my balance. I explained to the neurologist what my doctor had said and what I was doing to heal and that I would be starting physical therapy soon. The neurologist agreed that I needed physical therapy but advised me to stop taking Advil because she thought it was making my headaches worse. She recommended Tylenol instead. (Tylenol was not nearly strong enough, though, so I stopped taking pain medicine altogether and attempted to control the pain by not moving.) So after spending an entire day in the ER, we essentially did not walk away with any more answers than we had started with. I had secretly hoped that the doctors would find a little area that was bleeding. Then a quick surgery could fix it and I could get back to my life.

After the ER episode and two weeks of being off work completely, I began physical therapy. I was happy to finally be doing something other than sleeping. My first session was November 18 at 7 a.m. We scheduled my sessions for early morning so my husband could drop me off on his way to work. I remember walking into the Athletes' Training Center in Papillion, Nebraska, and feeling overwhelmed by the loud background music and bright lights. This was not going to be easy. I curled up in a chair in the waiting area with eyes pinched shut and hands over my ears. I felt like an autistic child wanting to crawl deep into my shell to escape all the stimuli. After a few minutes, my trainer came out and introduced herself to us. She quickly ushered me into a side room and closed the door so that I would be away from the background music and noise of the rest of the building. She also dimmed the lights for me. I was relieved that she understood what I was going through.

My physical therapist explained that our first session would consist of a baseline assessment of what I could do. She mentioned that she was on the same concussion team as my doctor and they worked together. She showed me diagrams of what happens when a concussion occurs and explained what we needed to work on. My brain was able to absorb only about half of what she said, but I got the gist of what she was saying. The focus of future physical therapy sessions would mostly be on restoring my balance, which was really out of whack. When I walked, I continued to feel like I was on the deck of a ship during a wicked storm.

Physical therapy was a saving grace in more ways than one. Twice a week I went to the Athletes' Training Center for hour-long sessions. I also had to do physical therapy at home at least twice a day. I was thrilled to have something to do during the day—finally! There was a chance I would retain my sanity after all. I walked heel-toe with my eyes closed for about 10 yards. I progressed to walking heel-toe with eyes open, looking side-to-side as I stepped. I also performed "eye push-ups" with beads on a string. I would set the timer for 30 seconds and then focus my eyes on individual beads on a string, each one a little further away, then closer. I had to do a series of about five exercises, three repetitions each. These exercises sound so simple now as I try to describe them, but there was nothing simple about them at the time. I had to concentrate and use all my cognitive energy to perform each task. Doing the exercises increased the feeling of pressure in my head, so it was important to take breaks. I sat down, closed my eyes and covered my ears for about five to ten minutes after doing each task. In order for physical therapy to be effective, we had to challenge my brain without straining it.

Physical therapy reignited my hope. I was starting to see some improvement with the simple exercises I was doing faithfully twice a day. My brain no longer needed to sleep quite as long during the day. Television was still intolerable, but I could read about five to ten minutes before I couldn't concentrate any longer. I needed to do something to stay sane, so I asked my husband to drive me to the local Michael's craft store. During college I used to hook rugs to relax between classes, and I thought this mindless task might be something my brain could tolerate. Walking was still draining, so my husband dropped me off at the store entrance and then parked the car. When I entered the store, the background music was too loud, the lights were too bright, and visual input from all the things on the shelves was completely overwhelming. Yikes! I didn't realize shopping would be so painful! I shuffled to the back of the store where the rug hooking kits were located and tried to make a selection as quickly as possible. There were just a few kits to choose from, but almost all were complicated. The "overwhelmed" warning light was blinking wildly in my head. Then I saw a simple kit that was just a big yellow smiley face like the "Have a Nice Day" faces of the '70s. I could do this one. It had only two colors and the message was upbeat. I needed all the positivity I could get.

So my days were filled with physical therapy exercises, resting, hooking a smiley face rug, resting, sleeping, and eating. I had developed a habit of grazing all day rather than eating big meals. Eating a big meal increased my symptoms. I remember my doctor advising me to eat light, and now I understood. She had also advised me to eat

Omega-3s, so I ate eggs daily and light salads with olive oil. I also nibbled on nuts. Constipation was still a problem since I could not exercise, so I ate roughage to compensate. I drank no alcohol and no caffeine because these substances interfere with the process of healing the brain. I was following all the rules in hopes of getting back to my life as quickly as possible, but a rapid recovery just wasn't in the cards.

Since I was home alone all day, it was easy to achieve silence. And the silence was a welcome balm for my concussed brain. No background music or TV noise. No conversations to overhear or participate in. Just silence. This much quiet would have been unsettling for the old me, but the concussed me readily welcomed it.

Thanksgiving was almost here—my favorite holiday. Traditionally my husband cooked a wonderful meal for our family. Each year my sister Deb and her family would come from Oconomowoc, Wisconsin and spend the entire weekend with us. We would play cards, watch movies, laugh and eat until we couldn't stand it anymore.

I had been phoning Deb regularly during my ordeal. I cried when I needed to cry. I tried not to cry much with Rick because I felt like I was already such a huge burden to him. Deb was my best friend as well as my sister, so she was a great sounding board for my frustrations with the slow healing process. She understood that I was still struggling and suggested that it might be better for me if her family not come to Omaha for Thanksgiving that year. I protested emphatically and insisted they come. I assured her I would be fine. My physical therapist also was concerned that the upcoming holiday festivities might be overwhelming for me. I assured her and my sister that I would faithfully take brain breaks. I would interact with people for 45 minutes, then take a brain break in my bedroom for 15 minutes. That was the plan.

Family from Wisconsin arrived; our adult children and grandchildren arrived. My husband baked homemade bread and pies the day before Thanksgiving in preparation for the big meal. It was all simultaneously wonderful and stressful. I wasn't stressed about hosting, but my brain was overwhelmed by all the stimuli. The feeling of a rubber band tightening around my head increased, my head hurt, and I couldn't think straight. But I refused to give up.

My then-four-year-old granddaughter, Annabeth, was curious about my head injury. She had called me "Bubbe" since she began to talk. I liked being called that; it somehow seemed endearing and appropriate. Besides, I felt too young to be called Grandma. We later learned that *Bubbe* is Yiddish for grandmother, which made me love the name all the more. Annabeth was not only a curious four-year-old but also quite chatty. When she insisted on taking breaks with her Bubbe during the Thanksgiving festivities, I couldn't say no. She would curl up beside me on my bed as I put the mask over my eyes and tried to quiet the buzzing and pain in my head. However, being four, she was not able to stop talking. I don't remember what she was talking about. I just remember it was nonstop chatter. So my "brain breaks" weren't exactly breaks and my symptoms worsened. I was finally rescued by Annabeth's mother, who realized what was happening and carried my granddaughter, against her protests, out of my room. I loved the fact that Annabeth wanted to be with me and comfort me. But sadly, I needed to be alone.

I managed to get through the holiday weekend. Family returned to their corners of the world and Rick returned to work. I returned to hooking my smiley face rug, doing physical therapy exercises, resting, reading a little, and resting some more. My condition was starting to improve. I could now sit in our sunny living room without needing to wear my eye mask to block the light. Weeks of physical therapy were greatly improving my balance. I was figuring out ways to accommodate my sensitive brain. I wore Rick's noise-cancelling earbuds in stores to make shopping tolerable. I could read simple text for about 10 to 15 minutes and maintain my focus and comprehension.

It was now December, and I was well enough to drive short distances. The Athletes' Training Center was conveniently located just a few miles from our house, so I drove myself to and from physical therapy sessions. The holidays were also approaching and so we had the usual tree and garland to put up as well as the annual Christmas letter and cards to get in the mail.

Although I was making progress, my recovery didn't seem to be happening quickly enough. I had begun to call my healing process "The Cha-Cha" because it was a constant two steps forward and one step back. Sometimes it was one step forward and two steps back. Every day was a battle with discouragement and feelings of hopelessness. My doctor checked in with me each time she saw me, concerned about my state of mind. I was aware that depression and even suicide risk were associated with prolonged concussion symptoms, but I was not depressed by medical standards. Although I had feelings of self-pity and hopelessness, I did not allow myself to feel that way for long. I would cry for a short time and then get on with it. I would do my physical therapy exercises, and I had started doing some light yoga in my living room as well. I had a catch phrase: "It could be worse." At least I wasn't dying! I remained hopeful by focusing on what I could do rather than what I could not do. I couldn't walk for more than 5 minutes without succumbing to exhaustion, and I certainly couldn't run yet. But I could do light yoga and I could hook a rug.

On the first Saturday in December, Rick brought the Christmas decorations out of the basement storage room. I had always loved this time of year and usually enjoyed making my house festive for the holidays. This year, however, decorating the house felt like an impossible mountain I had to climb. My husband would have done it for me in a heartbeat, but I insisted on doing it myself because I thought he wouldn't be able to do it to my satisfaction. I remember standing on our second-floor landing and hanging garlands. I had four strands to hang, and after the first one I felt awful—completely drained, head pressure mounting, yet unable to stop. I felt compelled to complete the task. Rick had gone to the store and

I wanted to finish before he returned. Instead of walking into the house and admiring the finished garland, Rick found me kneeling on the floor crying, "Make me stop; just make me stop." I couldn't do any more decorating, yet I couldn't stop myself from trying. I was completely exhausted and unable to function. My husband wrapped his loving arms around me and patiently guided me downstairs to the couch where I promptly curled up in the fetal position with my eye mask on and my ears covered. I needed a brain break!

On another December day I remember driving myself to our local Walgreens drugstore to order our Christmas cards. I strategically waited until just after I had eaten something and rested so I would have optimal energy to complete the mission. I had to get in and out quickly when shopping because it was an instant brain drain. As I stood at the kiosk selecting photos, I overheard a woman speaking to the store clerk. She was upbeat and looked so happy. But then I overheard her tell the clerk that her doctors had just informed her that there wasn't anything else they could do about her cancer and she had only a few months to live. She was planning a trip, I think, or maybe she was getting her photos from a trip she had already taken. I just remember her positive spirit and the way she shared her news. It was as if she had been set free to live her final days as she wanted. I returned to my car thinking, "If she can be that positive, then surely I can." And again the words "It could be worse" rang in my head. I clung to moments like these like rafts on a stormy sea. The Universe was reminding me to stay hopeful.

With the Christmas cards printed, now all I needed to do was check the annual letter that Rick wrote to complete our mailings to friends and family around the country. Rick's letter always summed up our year, described our grown children's year, and bragged about our granddaughters. He traditionally wrote the letter tongue-in-cheek, and most of our family and friends enjoyed a laugh from his creative, corny style. But 2014 had been a rough year for us. We had both lost our fathers and I had hit my head and become stuck in the rabbit hole of concussion recovery. This would be a difficult letter to write. In our Christmas letter-writing process, usually Rick wrote the letter and I did the final editing and printing. I opened the file of what he had written and couldn't believe what I was reading. His opening sentence was "This has been the worst year of our lives," and it didn't get any cheerier after that. There was no corny humor, just a raw, painful summary of our year. I couldn't stand the thought of sending out such a morose and depressing Christmas letter! So I spent a whole day, with breaks in between, channeling Rick's humor to rewrite our annual letter. Here is how "Rick" reported my concussion:

> *Sharon doesn't want me to tell you about her concussion—she'd rather forget about it! (Get it? Forget about it. Ha!) I just want you to know I had nothing to do with it. She bumped her head at work and now has lots of down time as she works on recovering. To pass the time, she has started to make latch hook rugs. I like to tell people that my wife bumped her head and became a hooker!*

Putting a positive spin on the situation wasn't easy, but it was the only way we were going to survive this challenge. Little did we know how much we would need our sense of humor in the years to come.

Soon it would be time for me to begin working half-days. I continued to pass the time with eye push-ups and heel-toe walking twice a day, along with some light yoga and napping. I continued hooking the smiley face rug, now able to do more than just a few rows at a time before quitting from exhaustion. I was also able to read for 15 minutes before needing a break. I began to read *Wild* by Cheryl Strayed. I found her story of struggling and literally climbing her way back to her life very cathartic. It was another raft of hope for me to cling to. Cheryl's story resonated strongly for me when she described the "jukebox in her head" as she hiked in silence along the Pacific Coast Trail. I had a jukebox in my head, too! Old '70s songs played randomly, especially when I would try to sleep. I often heard Carly Simon in my head singing, "I haven't got time for the pain."

On December 8 I returned to work part-time. Rick's employer, Union Pacific, had been more than generous by allowing him to have a flexible schedule. He was able to work in his office in the mornings, then work from home in the afternoons. The plan was for him to drop me off at school in the morning and then pick me up at noon to take me home so I could rest. Mornings were my best chance to be able to function at work. I should have been excited to return to school, but I felt incredibly anxious. I knew deep down I was not ready yet, but I wasn't about to be a wimp and give up. I had to try. Although I was just working half-days, I still needed brain breaks. I kept the fluorescent lights off in my office; big windows provided plenty of natural lighting. When I tried to walk around the building, I would become overwhelmed and almost disoriented, so I spent most of the time in my office. The lighting and sounds of an elementary school were a lot to take in. I just wasn't ready.

Unwilling to admit that I wasn't ready to handle the stress of working, I soldiered on. I would get through the mornings and collapse in utter exhaustion on the couch when I returned home. I slept most of the afternoon and was back to sleeping 11 to 12 hours a night. Returning to school was making my recovery go backwards. But I only needed to get through two weeks of school and then we would be on winter break, which would give me another two weeks to recover. I could make it.

An average day was too much for me, so I was really in trouble when stressful situations came up. One morning an angry parent came into the office and was yelling and screaming at my very competent secretary. This parent had some mental health issues and was known for her tirades. I remember sitting in my office and thinking I needed to go deal with this angry parent because my secretary was simply not paid enough to put up with that kind of abuse, although she was handling the situation very professionally. I walked out of my office into the main office area and it was like I had walked into a stone wall. I couldn't talk or move. The sound of the yelling parent and brightness of the fluorescent lighting in the main office area overwhelmed me. I was frozen. I looked at the parent and my secretary and then cowered back into my office for relief. I had my wits about me enough to realize that being at work in my condition was possibly more of a liability than a help. After the parent had left and the office was quiet again, I walked out to speak to my secretary. I couldn't find the words to explain what had happened to me, so I just started crying and told her I was sorry. She hugged me, but I could tell she did not understand. A person with a concussion looks normal, so people expect you to act and be normal. But a concussed brain is anything but normal.

Although I was unable to deal with stress or the day-to-day responsibilities of running a large elementary school, I soldiered on. I did not want anyone to think I couldn't do my job, especially me. In hindsight my decision to stay at work was quite selfish.

Our school held its annual winter concert in the morning on the last Wednesday before winter break. Our program was scheduled so that each class would come to the stage, sing their three songs, and then return to the classroom. Any veering from the daily routine could throw off some of our most vulnerable students, so we strategically stuck to the daily lessons and schedules aside from the singing on stage. Our auditorium was filled with proud parents and I was sitting at the back of the room with my noise-cancelling earbuds in, trying to endure all the sounds and stimuli. I kept checking the time: just two hours to go before Rick would take me home. I could make it. We were about halfway through the concert when a parent, her mother, and her toddler walked by me. I knew her son was in the second grade and had already sung, so I greeted her and politely told her that her son's class had already performed. But I also told her that the concert would be repeated in the afternoon so she was welcome to come back and see him then. This parent and I had a rough history, and she, too, was known for her tirades. I was trying to keep her calm as she learned that she had missed her son's performance. She insisted that she needed to see him at that moment. I explained to her that he was in class with his teacher, but that his lunch was scheduled in just 20 minutes and she was welcome to stay and eat lunch with him. At this point we were standing in the hallway having this discussion so that we wouldn't interrupt the concert. The more I asked her to wait and not interrupt her son's class, the more insistent she became. Her son's class was directly across the hall from the auditorium, so we could see through the glass window in the door that the teacher was leading a small reading group at her kidney-shaped table and the other students were quietly working. I repeated to this parent that walking in with her toddler would be an unnecessary disruption and asked her not to go into the classroom. She started talking excitedly to her mother, who was trying hard to calm her down and defuse the situation. As she spoke to her mother, the kindergarten students were walking by us on their way to perform in the auditorium. I turned to hug, high-five, and wish the little ones good luck. When I pivoted back around, the parent was gone. Against my wishes, she had entered the classroom and was standing over the seated teacher talking to her. My reaction was not good. Controlling emotions when a brain is concussed is enormously difficult, if not impossible. Like a runaway train, once the emotions start up there is no stopping them and they seem to just gain momentum. I went into the classroom and told the parent, "I specifically asked you not to do this; now you need to leave."

This approach was confrontational and not the best way to handle the situation, but it was all I could manage at the time. The parent did leave the room, but outside the closed door she got very close to my face and began yelling at me. I remember grabbing my ears, again like an autistic child who couldn't take it anymore, and repeatedly asking her to stop. I even said I had a head injury and she was making my head hurt. But all of this just seemed to fuel the situation more. I had my walkie-talkie on, so I called for security. The parent called me a racist bitch as she was led out the door. My energy level had drained down to zero, and I needed to go home and recharge.

Now there were only two mornings left before break, and I was going to do this come hell or high water. I received a phone call from the central office. The angry parent that I had escorted out of the building had gone straight to the superintendent's office to complain about me. I was instructed to meet with the parent, but I did not have the cognitive or emotional stamina to meet with her. It was physically impossible. I called my direct supervisor and asked him to meet with the parent for me. He was the executive director (ED), a new position in the district. Principals were told that our EDs were there to support us, so I sought support. The executive directors were told they were there to coach us, so he sought to coach. When I asked him to meet with this parent, his response was "And how will that solve the problem?" I tried to explain that I wasn't physically capable of handling this volatile situation, but I was doing it badly. All that I could get out of my mouth was "This isn't a race issue!" The angry parent was African American, as was my ED. To them this was most certainly a race issue, and understandably so. But for me it was a health issue. I was simply not capable. After being told I had to meet with this parent, I shot off an emotional email to my ED and the superintendent. I told them that I had sacrificed my health for my job long enough and I couldn't do it anymore. I don't think they had any idea what I was talking about. I'm sure I sounded like I was having a tirade of my own. But the new superintendent and executive director did not know me well enough to understand that this type of response was out of character for me.

Before leaving the school building for winter break, I called Human Resources and asked to speak with the Assistant Superintendent of HR. Thankfully, she was available and took my call right away. Again, I was unable to keep my emotions in check. I started crying and could barely speak. I told her between sobs that I was trying my best to both do my job and heal my head but I couldn't do both without help. When I tearfully asked for help, her first response was to ask where my executive director was. I responded, "I don't know, and I don't think he gets it." As I continued to cry like a baby into the phone, she patiently listened and calmed me down. She reassured me that the school district would hire a retired principal to work alongside me for as long as I needed. She asked for time to make the arrangements, since winter break was just a day away. I was so grateful! For the first time I felt heard. I felt understood. I was relieved. I could make it one more day and then rest up during the two-week break.

I made it to the break, but two weeks of half-days had caused me to slip back down deeper into the rabbit hole again. I had an appointment with a neuropsychologist during winter break. Back in October, my physician had referred me to her because she thought it would be wise for me to undergo a neuropsychological assessment and get some more specific brain exercises to help my healing process. However, there were only a few neuropsychologists in Omaha, so I could not get an appointment to see her until the end of the year. I was instructed to schedule the appointment for first thing in the morning so my brain would be fresh.

The neuropsychologist performed a variety of tests, providing brain breaks for me in between. The tests mainly assessed my memory, response time, and perception of spatial relationships. After over two hours of testing, I was exhausted. The doctor asked me to schedule a follow-up visit to finish the assessment since she did not want to test me when my brain was fatigued. Because all the assessing occurred in the morning and after several days off work, I was able to do reasonably well. I was told that I had tested in the normal range for my age for everything but response time and spatial relationship stuff. The "for my age" qualifier stung a bit. What was that supposed to mean? I thought it would have made more sense to test me in the afternoon when I really struggled. My brain functioned much more slowly as the day wore on. My brain was like a cell phone battery that is going bad: when you plug it in, it charges and functions fine, but then it loses its charge very quickly. So assessing me while my brain was fully charged was pointless! And despite that "for your age" business, I knew I was capable of better performance.

4

Work Stress and Coming Out of the Closet

My doctor was going on maternity leave after the first of the year. Before going on leave, she had written a note for me to remain on half-days for the first two weeks of January and instructed me to contact her colleague if I needed anything. She said she would inform him of my case.

The first day back at school after winter break was a teacher work day with no students. I only had to make it through the morning. But even on this easy day the stress of piled-up emails, teachers needing support, fluorescent lights, copy machines whirling, and phones ringing set me back quickly. The rubber band tightened around my head, my anxiety rose, and I lost my ability to focus and think clearly. It was obvious that I would need more than two weeks on half-days. I probably shouldn't have been working at all, but someone had to steer the ship. I called my doctor's office and made an appointment for that Friday with her colleague.

I waited in the exam room for the doctor to see me. He entered hurriedly, and I don't remember him even establishing eye contact with me. I told him that I was the patient with a concussion. He responded bluntly, "She has lots of patients with concussions. What do you need?" I explained that I didn't feel ready to return to work full-time, and he asked how much time I thought I needed. I said, "Two more weeks of partial days." He quickly wrote on his notepad, "Needs to continue working partial days for two more weeks, with frequent breaks as needed." He tore the note from his pad and left the exam room. I really missed my own doctor!

I decided I would have to get strategic about accommodating my head if I was going to continue trying to work. I brought a lawn chair with a reclining back and a small footstool to work. I had a little walk-in coat closet in my office that I cleared for the chair and stool. I scheduled 10-minute breaks every hour and disciplined myself to take them, even if I was in the middle of something. I didn't adhere to my schedule perfectly, but I tried. It took all of my self-discipline to stop for breaks, yet the breaks felt so good! There wasn't any lighting in the closet, so when I went in and closed the door I was in complete darkness. I could still hear the secretaries' voices and phones ringing in the main office area, so I plugged my ears as I reclined in my lawn chair in the darkness. I craved nothingness. I needed nothingness. The whirly-twirly Flash had been brought to her knees and now had no choice but to be still.

Human Resources kept their promise and sent a wonderful retired principal to work alongside me. In reality, she did all the heavy lifting while I did what I could from my office. For example, she supervised the lunchroom. I could barely walk into the cafeteria because the lighting and multiple conversations completely overwhelmed me. My filter was still broken and I could not tune out background noise.

In addition, it was time to play catch-up with formal observations of the teachers. These observations generally took between 30 and 60 minutes. I had over twenty teachers to observe, and many of them needed three observations that year. Formal observations of teachers required sitting in the classroom and observing a lesson while taking detailed notes that would serve as a basis for meaningful feedback. The multi-tasking involved in watching a teacher teach, listening to his or her words, observing students' responses, and simultaneously taking notes was more than my concussed brain could handle. So the retired principal who had been sent by HR took care of all the formal observations and conferences for me. I am forever in her debt for stepping in and leading when I was not able. Thank you, Kathy Nelson!

Humor continued to help me to stay sane. My office staff was well aware of my breaks in the closet. If they couldn't find me, they knew where I was. They had lots of laughs talking about Sharon coming out of the closet! When the staff saw my husband's car arrive to take me home at noon each day, they would call out, "Sharon, your day care van is here!" It was funny, and I appreciated the comic relief.

January was a turning point for me. Although I was receiving support from another principal, taking breaks, and only working partial days, I felt my healing process was stalled at best, if not going backwards. I had no physical or mental stamina, and the simplest tasks drained me. Heavy fatigue and head pressure were my primary symptoms at this point, along with continued sensitivity to noise and light. I could function fairly normally for short periods but had to return to the dark, silent closet often to recharge my brain.

I was determined to get out of the rabbit hole. One day I Googled "post-concussion syndrome" for the millionth time, looking for the magic bullet that would cure me. I came across a wonderful site called Healyourconcussion.com. It had been created by a woman who was studying nutrition and had a car accident that caused a concussion. She, too, had fallen into the rabbit hole of post-concussion syndrome. The site was designed to be user-friendly for someone with a head injury. It had simple text with large, simple pictures. Lucy, the creator of the site, had basically developed a survival guide for anyone with post-concussion syndrome. I already knew about the importance of avoiding alcohol and caffeine completely and eating light and healthy, low-salt meals. But even though I was following all the rules, I was still stuck. Lucy provided a list of vitamins and supplements that she recommended for people with PCS. Maybe I had found the silver bullet I was looking for! With the list of supplements in hand, my husband drove me to the local natural foods store and we filled our shopping basket with over $200 worth of supplements. They included:

1. Melatonin in liquid form to help get my sleep pattern back to normal

2. CoQ10 and resveratrol to restore cellular health and function

3. Turmeric as a natural anti-inflammatory

4. 800 mg capsules of Norwegian fish oil for Omega 3 fatty acids

5. BioplasmaTM cell salts for cellular health and function

The information from Healyourconcussion.com and the supplements were a real turning point for me. I was sleeping better and my energy was improving. I kept the bottle of Bioplasma cell salts next to my computer at work and sucked on those little tablets all day long. I am still not sure whether my condition was improving because I was finally sleeping better, because I was doing something to aid my healing besides waiting, or because the supplements actually worked. I didn't care if it was a placebo effect—anything that gave me relief from the fatigue and head pressure was welcomed.

Prior to beginning my supplement regime, each day was a huge struggle to not only keep my energy levels up but my spirits as well. Depression and anxiety are common with concussions, and I was acutely aware that they were the other dragons I had to slay. I had always benefited from reading for inspiration, so to battle the feelings of depression and anxiety I began to read Deepak Chopra's *The Seven Spiritual Laws of Success*. I don't remember how I came across the book, but it was short with not too many words on each page and looked simple enough for my brain to comprehend. Although the title was about success, the book really was about finding happiness and contentment—two things I hadn't felt since my head injury.

At the end of each chapter, the book provided suggestions for applying the various "laws" described. In the chapter on "The Law of Least Effort," Deepak writes,

> *Today I will practice acceptance. I will know that this moment is as it should be, because the whole universe is as it should be. I will not struggle against the whole universe by struggling against this moment. My acceptance is total and complete. I accept things as they are this moment, not as I wish they were.*

I realized as I read these words that I had to let go and stop trying so hard—I had to stop fighting my concussion. This type of acceptance went against my nature and contradicted everything

I had done to survive in my life. Yet this simple notion of acceptance brought me to tears. Reading these words over and over, I felt relieved of the burden of fighting my concussion. I printed the words and put them on my kitchen calendar to read every morning before starting my day. They brought me immense comfort and were a daily reminder to accept, for now, my concussion.

In addition to taking supplements, improving my sleep patterns, and accepting my situation for the moment, I also began to keep a gratitude journal. I remembered hearing Oprah describe a time when she was discouraged and she was telling Maya Angelou, her dear friend and mentor, about her troubles. Dr. Angelou's response was to advise Oprah to stop and be grateful for the situation—to simply give thanks. I wasn't feeling particularly grateful, but I thought it was worth a shot. With my noise-cancelling earbuds in place, I went to Target and bought a pretty journal to use as I began documenting what I was thankful for each day. Here are excerpts from my first two entries:

January 14

1. Trip to Target with my loving daughter, Mary, to buy this journal. We had a great chat.

2. The talk with the angry parent at school went exceedingly well. Had an epiphany about my boss. I was taking his actions personally when in fact he is just inexperienced. It was very freeing to realize it's not about me!

3. "Donuts with the Principal" went well this morning. Had 11 parents attend, and they spoke up about issues that concerned them. I am glad my parents are beginning to feel empowered!

4. My loving husband went grocery shopping tonight so I didn't have to. He's quite a guy!

5. Dinner conversation with my son Joe. I told him about my day at work and he was a very attentive listener (probably more attentive than people without Asperger's!).

6. Beautiful sunset that I was home in time to enjoy. Temperatures warming over the next few days. Grateful for the mini-thaw in the midst of winter.

January 15

1. A great night's sleep!
2. Beautiful sunrise and warmer temps
3. Smooth Kindergarten Round-Up
4. First-grader who asked if my head was better yet. I replied, "almost." And she said, "Ah...I wanted it to be better today!" And I said, "I wanted it to be better yesterday!" Loved her hug!

I thought my healing process was moving in the right direction, yet I continued to have huge setbacks. I continued using my upbeat strategies: popping supplements, accepting my condition (more or less), journaling, and taking brain breaks. I was taking 2400 mg of fish oil daily. I thought surely I would sprout gills! But it was easy to get discouraged when I was having what I called bad head days. Bad head days usually occurred when I had not slept well the night before. Sleep is crucial to healing the brain after a concussion. Paradoxically, the concussed brain has a difficult time sleeping. Again I turned to Deepak Chopra for help. He suggested using a sleeping mantra to drift into sleep. This mantra was not created specifically for people with head injuries, but I was willing to try anything. The mantra was "Om Agasthi Shahina" (OHM ah-gah-stee SHAH-ee-nah). I had to keep a printed copy of the mantra on the nightstand next to my bed because I couldn't remember the damned thing! But when my head would not allow me to settle down to sleep, I would use the mantra. It helped, but it wasn't a magic bullet. Sleep issues continued, but I soldiered on, sure that I would wake up one day soon and this nightmare would be over.

5

God's Foot on My Forehead

Principals were required to attend monthly administrators' meetings at the central office building in downtown Omaha. These meetings usually lasted 3 to 4 hours and were held in the boardroom, which was a large space with many fluorescent lights. I was nervous about attending the first meeting since my concussion. Although I was working full days, I wasn't driving myself to work yet and I didn't know how I would get from the central office back to school. I also didn't know how I was going to handle the fluorescent lights and all the talking for hours on end. Regardless, I had my husband drop me off at the central office building and figured I would just ask a colleague for a ride back to school.

As I walked into the large boardroom, I was overwhelmed by all the mini-conversations that were taking place before the meeting had even started. The lighting was immediately irritating and the Curriculum and Learning Department was playing rock music LOUDLY to motivate us. I was trying to be inconspicuous, but I couldn't take it. I put on my noise-cancelling earbuds and felt some relief. I should have put my sunglasses on to shield my eyes from the harsh lighting, but I didn't want to call attention to myself.

I would have been less embarrassed if I'd had some dramatic story to explain how I got the concussion. If I had been in a horrible car accident, let's say, or had fallen from a ladder, or had even been hit in the head by an angry parent, I would not have hesitated to put on sunglasses to protect my eyes during that meeting. I was embarrassed that all I had done was hit my head on a cabinet door.

The meeting began and speakers were using microphones—an immediate assault on my ears and head! I couldn't concentrate to comprehend the information they were sharing. I left the room several times and sat on a bench that was just outside the boardroom. Ahhh... relief! A few passersby saw me sitting on the bench and asked if I was okay. I simply replied that I was taking a short brain break. The whole process was so draining that

I got nothing out of the meeting because I couldn't comprehend what the speakers were saying. But at least I had attended the required meeting. Baby steps were better than no steps at all. A gracious colleague who was also a principal in South Omaha near Indian Hill agreed to give me a ride back to school. She was very caring and sympathetic, and I greatly appreciated her empathy.

Stress from attending the meeting and returning to full days of work sent me sliding back down into the rabbit hole. Lights and sounds became overwhelming again. A high-pitched buzzing was ever-present in my head, along with a feeling of vise grips squeezing tightly around my brain. The pain was mostly a dull ache and didn't bother me nearly as much as the squeezing sensation. The return of extreme fatigue was overwhelming and discouraging. Even with frequent breaks, I could barely manage to get through the workday and then I would come home and crash. My husband fed me and tucked me into bed. I was usually asleep by 7:00 p.m. in order to get up at 6:00 the next morning and do it all again. But now President's Day weekend had arrived and I would have three full days to recharge my batteries.

Often when people have chronic health issues or have undergone a traumatic loss, they start blaming themselves. Sheryl Sandberg describes this phenomenon in her book *Option B: Facing Adversity, Building Resilience, and Finding Joy*. Sandberg describes "personalization" as the belief that we are at fault for our loss or chronic health issue. Although logically and in every other way I did not believe that God or the Universe was vindictive or angrily punishing people, I started to slip into a mindset of feeling punished. I felt as though I had been climbing a steep mountain, arriving at the top and feeling God's foot pressing on my forehead and pushing me back down while commanding, "Climb again! You still don't get it!"

My self-blame went back to a promise I had made but not yet fulfilled. My father had passed away exactly one year earlier on President's Day. We had moved him from Arizona to Nebraska to be near us as he aged. For the majority of his seven years in Omaha he was able to live happily and reasonably independently in senior living apartments. However, during his final year his cognitive skills declined sharply and he lost weight at a rapid rate. He had become paranoid about food and would not eat. His assisted living facility was not staffed to provide the care he needed, so the social worker met with me and advised me to find a nursing home. My father was not a rich man. He had been a simple factory worker who eked out a living for his family of six by living paycheck to paycheck. His savings were depleted, and his only resources were his monthly social security checks and Medicaid. His financial situation greatly reduced our options for care facilities.

I remembered one facility, Montclair Nursing Home, where our church had sung Christmas carols several years previously. I remembered thinking at the time that it seemed like a very warm and homey place. With that memory in mind, I called Montclair for my dad and was told that they had an opening. I asked to tour the facility and made the appointment for 7:00 a.m. the next day so I could stop by for a tour before work. That was mistake number one. At 7:00 a.m. most of the residents were still sleeping. Everything was quiet, peaceful, and immaculate. I explained to the intake administrator that the main reason Dad needed extra care was that he wasn't eating. She reassured me that they would have an aide sit with Dad at every meal and make sure he ate. Montclair was just ten minutes from my home and right on my way to work. They had an opening and took Medicaid patients. It seemed perfect, so we moved Dad to Montclair immediately.

Things are not always as they seem, however, and to say that things at Montclair were less than perfect would have been a huge understatement. My father left the facility in an ambulance only six weeks after moving in, never to return.

When he died, I promised myself and my siblings that I would do something about the conditions at Montclair. I obtained the name of the mega-corporation in Florida that owned and operated the facility. I put the information in the basket where I file bills and important documents, but I didn't take action. The contact information sat in my basket for a full year.

My father's death was a reminder to my husband Rick that his own father would not live forever. Emil was 93 years old and holding his own in Dayton, Ohio. It's not easy to get from Omaha to Dayton, so sometimes years had passed between Rick's trips to visit his parents. We decided to use spring break to drive to Dayton.

It was March 2014, just one month since my father had passed away. We were driving east on Interstate 80 when Rick's cell phone rang. It was his mother. She sounded frantic and said an ambulance was on its way to their house. Emil had fallen and apparently hit his head.

Rick's parents had been married their whole lives. She was a war bride who had been only 15 years old when they met. He was a handsome, young soldier going off to fight in WWII. Her husband was her everything, and she did not know how to let him go. So after months of painful discussions and sometimes disagreements about what was best for Emil, he left this world and his family struggled greatly with their loss. My husband had been very close to his father, in his own way. So after my father-in-law's death my focus was on yet another loss and supporting my husband.

Once a month I took out my basket of bills to pay and saw the handwritten note with the name and address of the corporation that owned Montclair. Each time I looked at the note I sat frozen, unable to take steps to fulfill my promise to do something about the poor care my father had received.

Only sixteen days after we buried my father-in-law, I hit my head on the cabinet door and started my journey down the rabbit hole. So on this President's Day, five months into my concussion recovery, I found myself bargaining with God. I knew that God was not punishing me, but desperation and despair does funny things to one's thinking. I just wanted His foot off my head.

It was a bright, sunny day. The light was mildly irritating as I sat in my home office and pulled up Pink's song, "Beam Me Up" on YouTube. We had played the song at my dad's funeral service, with pictures of his grandchildren and great-grandchildren playing on the screen in the background. So it seemed appropriate to listen to the song on this day, the anniversary of his death. There is a line in the song that encapsulated exactly how I was feeling: "I want to feel lighter, I'm tired of being a fighter I think, just beam me up..." Those words now held a different meaning for me than they had held a year ago. At that time I had related them to how Dad had felt when he said, "I've lived my life; just let me go." But after five months of struggling with a concussion it was I who wanted to feel lighter because I was tired of fighting my way out of the rabbit hole.

So with that mindset I began my negotiation with God. It went something like this:

"Okay, God, I broke my promise. I did not contact the owners of Montclair and I did not do anything about the appalling conditions of the facility my father was in. You won't let me out of the rabbit hole I am trapped in until I fulfill my promise. Is that it? Well, I'm going to fix that right now!"

I then turned to my computer and composed the following letter:

February 17, 2015

To Whom It May Concern,

I am writing to tell you a sad story. My father, John Barrett, died one year ago today. He was 87 years old and had been moved from his assisted living facility to Montclair Nursing Home in Omaha, Nebraska. Your company owns Montclair. He was moved because he was no longer eating and his dementia had increased. He was losing weight quickly and was just not eating. His previous facility did not have the resources to have someone sit with him at meals and make sure he ate. Under their advisement, we moved him to a nursing home, presumably for better care.

We moved my father to Montclair Nursing Home the third week of November, 2013. I live nearby and was able to stop in often. My first concern was when I came to visit him at dinner time and he was not in the dining room. I went to his room and found him sitting alone in his chair with his pants undone, just sitting there (highly unusual and not like him at all). When I asked, "Pops, why aren't you going to dinner?" he simply replied, "They never came to get me."

I spoke to the manager and reminded him that one of the main reasons my father had been moved to Montclair was because he wasn't eating and that I had been assured the staff would make sure he ate. They didn't even make sure he was in the dining room.

I met with Montclair's manager, social workers, and nurse manager as my list of concerns continued to grow. He was not bathed nor shaved for over a week. I was reassured that my father would be well taken care of and that my list of concerns would be addressed. I saw no improvement whatsoever, and in fact, the very next week I received multiple phone calls reporting that my father had fallen. When I went to check on him, he had a very big black eye.

On January 3, 2014, just six weeks after moving my father to Montclair, I received a phone call from the staff notifying me that he had fallen again and they were calling the squad to take him to a nearby hospital. That call was received at about 10:00 a.m. He was not transported to the hospital until after 1:00 p.m. When I arrived at the emergency room, my father was in enormous pain. He reported to me that he had fallen at the facility because he

needed to use the restroom and called for help, but no one came. He couldn't wait any longer, so he tried to go by himself. When he fell, his bladder burst because it was so full. Emergency surgery was performed. He survived the surgery very well and was doing fine for about three days. Then when physical therapists came to get him up and moving, he refused to work with them. He decided that he had lived his life and he no longer wanted to try to heal. He was moved to a lovely facility called the Josie Harper Hospice House where he died three weeks later. Thanks to the care he received at the Hospice House, he at least was able to die with dignity.

My father's six weeks in your facility was an absolute nightmare. I am writing to appeal to your humanity and ask you to simply do a better job of providing care to our vulnerable elderly. I did not write sooner because my grief was so great that I felt literally frozen. But for the sake of my father's memory and for all others who enter the doors of Montclair Nursing Home, I hope and pray you will put systems in place to monitor the quality of care and ensure that all who live in your facilities are cared for with respect and dignity.

It is my hope that someone with a soul who has compassion in your organization will read this letter and take action.

Sincerely,

Sharon Royers

I did not expect a response when I mailed the letter to the mega-corporation's headquarters in Florida. But to my surprise, about two weeks later I received a heartfelt email from the district manager. He explained that they had become aware of problems with Montclair prior to receiving my letter. They were in the process of replacing the manager and much of the staff. He asked me to give him about a month to turn things around and then he wanted me to visit the facility to see the improvements. He also requested that I speak to the staff so they could hear my father's story. I agreed to speak in March or April.

I was fulfilling my promise. That should do it. The Foot should be released from my forehead any minute now and I could get back to my life. Back to being the Flash. But that's not what happened.

6

Still Doing the Cha-Cha

It was now March of 2015, six months into concussion recovery. I remembered reading on a website that it sometimes takes three months, six months, or even a year for people to fully recover from a concussion. So after passing the three-month mark, I was looking forward to six months with optimistic anticipation. I woke up each morning expecting to be magically better and back to my old self. The self that had enough energy to wake early and go for a run. The self that had so much energy she could light up a room. The self that rarely felt tired. I missed her.

I was still working full days and driving myself to and from school Monday through Thursday. However, by Friday my mental and physical energy were depleted, so my husband drove me to work the last day of each week. Old me used to love my 30-minute commute to work. I would blast old-school rock music and sing at the top of my lungs. Bob Seger and I would duet "On a long and lonesome highway, east of Omaha..." Singing helped energize and psych me up for the day ahead. But the concussed me was unable to drive and listen to the radio at the same time. Even soft, quiet music while driving was irritating. My brain could not handle it because it took all my cognitive energy to concentrate on driving.

Multi-tasking was impossible when I tried to cook as well. I have never really enjoyed cooking, but my husband does and is excellent at it. I tell everyone I married Rick for his cooking. However, I did enjoy baking on occasion and I made a pretty mean cookie. Old me loved listening to music while baking. Bette Midler, The Eagles, Kansas all accompanied me while I made chocolate chip or holiday cookies for my family. I had read on another concussion recovery website that following a recipe was good therapy, so I tried to bake. I discovered that I could not listen to music and follow a recipe at the same time. It was absolutely impossible. I couldn't even carry on a conversation while baking. It took 100% of my concentration and cognitive energy to bake. As long as there were no distractions I could follow a recipe—one I had been using for over 30 years. However, I felt like I had just run a marathon by the time I was done. It completely exhausted me. Everything I loved to do exhausted me. That was the paradox I was living. I needed to remain hopeful and keep my spirits up. But everything I loved to do would stress my concussed brain. How was I going to survive this?

Though it was draining, I continued trying to exercise. I would walk about a third of what used to be my running route. I couldn't even finish that much, and I was walking at a snail's pace. There are benches in the park and along the Zorinsky Lake trail, and often I needed to stop and sit for 5 to 10 minutes and rest before I could work up the energy to continue walking. It was so frustrating! My leg muscles, my heart, and my lungs all felt fine and wanted to forge ahead at a rapid pace, but my head would not allow us to do that.

Throughout my recovery process, I read when I was able. I chose books that were not too complicated and yet inspiring. One such book was Tom Brokaw's *A Lucky Life Interrupted*. I had always loved Tom Brokaw, and in this age of questionable journalism I respected and appreciated him even more. In his book, Mr. Brokaw described his cancer diagnosis and his struggle physically, mentally, and spiritually with his recovery process. He, too, was unable to exercise the way he used to do. He described looking at a life-sized poster of Tom Brady across from his New York apartment. Brady was a relatively young, healthy athlete able to physically do whatever he wanted to do, pain-free. Mr. Brokaw looked at Brady's picture and thought, "F--- you!" He referred to it as his therapeutic moment. I laughed at this anecdote because I had the same thought every time a runner would pass me on the trail as I shuffled along like a 90-year-old woman. If super-nice guy Tom Brokaw could think "F--- you," so could I.

Whenever I was attempting to walk for exercise, the squeezing sensation in my head increased as my heart rate went up. Additionally, my heart rate seemed to jump from a normal rate to high much too quickly. After I shared this information with my husband, he suggested we purchase a heart rate monitor. He researched for me and we decided to buy a Garmin, the kind with a wrist unit that syncs with a band you put around your chest. I began to wear my Garmin when I went on my attempted exercise walks. By the time I had shuffled about one block toward the trail my heart rate was already at 90. Ninety was the point when the rubber band tightened around my head and began squeezing. If I did not pay attention to this squeezing an elephant would land on my head, creating an extremely painful headache. Despite knowing this, I would push on. I kept thinking that I wasn't even on the route I used to run yet. I was just getting to the trail. And I was moving at a geriatric pace! No, I had to push on even though my Garmin and my head warned me not to.

As I mentioned earlier, I had nicknamed my recovery process "The Cha-Cha." The name seemed appropriate because I was always taking two steps forward and one step back. Sometimes it was one step forward, two steps back. After weeks of attempting to "exercise walk," I figured out I was trying to walk too far too soon. I stopped focusing on returning to my old running route and began to focus on what I was able to do with only a minimal increase in symptoms. We live on a dead-end street with several cul-de-sacs. I noticed that it took me about 5 minutes to walk one cul-de-sac. I started to just walk one. I did this for about a week with a minimal increase in head pressure. Then I added another cul-de-sac. I could do this with a minimal increase in symptoms. I continued this strategy of focusing on what I was able to do comfortably instead of pushing myself to do more. After weeks of this I was actually able to walk three cul-de-sacs. Fifteen minutes of walking (slowly) with very little increase in head pressure. I was making progress.

At about this time my energy and stamina began to improve noticeably. I was able to drive myself to and from work on Fridays again. It was still exhausting, but I could do it. My doctor had returned from her maternity leave, so I scheduled a visit. During my check-up I told her that my condition was improving and I had returned to work full-time, but I still didn't feel like myself. My stamina was increasing but remained very low compared to that of the Flash, and I really couldn't exercise. My 15-minute "exercise walks" were still very geriatric. Although I was able to get through the workday, I felt exhausted by the end of the day and slept 11 hours at night, once I was able to fall asleep. My doctor's response to all this was to remind me that my age was a factor in my recovery. (This was not something that I wanted to hear!) When I mentioned the heart rate issue in particular and how my brain just did not tolerate an increase in heart rate over 90, she responded by telling me that there was simply no research to verify that. I didn't say it out loud, but in my head I thought, "F*** the research!" I knew my body, and I knew that increasing my heart rate would intensify my symptoms. But I smiled and listened to her suggestions. It wasn't that she didn't believe me; she just had another theory about why I couldn't tolerate exercise. She thought I still had ocular-motor issues and set me up with the concussion clinic at the Nebraska Medical Center. Although deep down I knew the problem was related to my heart rate, I was still relieved to try something new. It renewed my hope that I could get off the latest plateau I was stuck on.

In the meantime, I still needed to fulfill my promise to visit Montclair and share my dad's story with their new and improved staff. When they had invited me back in February I had immediately picked up my phone and called my sister, Deb. She and I are very close. Though eighteen months apart in age, we are more like twins. We're connected in ways that can't be explained. We finish each other's sentences; we read each other's minds. We can just look at each other and break out laughing—often to the point of wetting our pants. I can't attend church with her anymore because inevitably we will start laughing uncontrollably. I was there for her when she went through her breast cancer ordeal, and she would be there for me as I wound my way through the labyrinth of concussion recovery.

Although Deb lived in Wisconsin and led a busy life as a special education teacher, she did not hesitate to say yes when I asked her to come to Omaha and join me in making a presentation to the Montclair staff. Throughout my career I had made numerous presentations and led countless professional development sessions and staff meetings. I was an adjunct instructor at two universities. I was not afraid of public speaking, but I knew that I did not have the emotional, physical, or cognitive stamina to articulate Dad's story by myself.

As anticipated, Deb was a huge help. She flew into Omaha the day before our scheduled presentation. We gathered a few pictures of Mom and Dad on their wedding day and with their children and grandchildren. We wanted to remind the staff that the aged and broken bodies they cared for had led previous lives. Vibrant, happy, healthy lives. We all age if we're lucky enough to do so, and the caretakers of the elderly have a sacred task. That was our basic message.

We were scheduled to speak to the staff at 10:30 a.m. on Monday, March 2. We walked into Montclair and immediately noticed the changes the staff had made. The facility had always been clean, but now it appeared warmer and more friendly. We were greeted at the front door by the district manager. Before our presentation, he took the time to proudly show us around the facility. They had fired the old manager and hired a new one, a retired nun. Half the staff had been let go and new staff were hired and trained. I was relieved to see that these much-needed improvements had been made.

After the tour of the facility, we were led to a conference room where staff meetings were held. There, sitting around the table, were the majority of the staff. They looked a little nervous. Deb spoke first and shared photos of our parents. She emphasized the importance and sacredness of their jobs, caring for our most vulnerable elderly. Together we told our parents' story of working hard and raising four children. Our intent was to personalize the story so they could relate to it. After Deb shared our past, I tearfully shared the details of my dad's experience in their facility. By the time we were finished speaking, there wasn't a dry eye in the room. We had touched their hearts as intended. The district manager made an impromptu decision. He announced that they would be renaming the conference room in our dad's honor. It would be the John Barrett Conference Room as a reminder to staff of the importance of their caretaking not only to the elderly but to their families as well. We were invited to return at a later date after they had installed the plaque with Dad's name on it on the door.

Atonement. Vindication. Price paid. I had done all that I knew how to do. I had regained my senses by this point, however, and no longer related the pace of my healing process to punishment or rewards from a higher power. In my heart I knew that the Creator of the Universe is loving, not vindictive. In fact, my personal definition of God is literally love: God is love. Love does not punish or seek vengeance. Sometimes bad things just happen.

It was now May of 2015 and the school year was drawing to a close. I was feeling much stronger than I had felt in January, but I wasn't quite out of the rabbit hole yet. I still needed to go into my dark closet at work for brain breaks. I still needed 10 to 11 hours of sleep each night. My brain still couldn't tolerate my heart rate increasing past 90. I still needed to be ever-mindful of living with my brakes on, careful not to overdo anything. I was eager for summer to arrive so I could focus 100% on healing and finally be done with this concussion nonsense!

That Mother's Day, before summer began, my family made an extra effort to make the day special for me. They knew I was going through a lot and struggling daily to stay positive and upbeat. So they got together before Mother's Day and planned a surprise. They had bought a two-man kayak, complete with life jackets and cooler. Now my husband and I could go out on Zorinsky Lake and enjoy the peaceful waters. And since it was a two-man kayak, I wouldn't even have to paddle! Exercising in the great outdoors would give me a glimpse of my former self. The kayak was a symbol of hope.

7

Hope in George Clooney's Eyes

I was one week into my summer of resting and recovering. I had returned to occupational and physical therapy at the Nebraska Medical Center. The concussion team had evaluated me and decided that my family physician was right—I still had ocular motor issues. Essentially they determined that my eyes were not working together. They explained to me that no one's eyes work perfectly together, but normally our brains compensate for the subtle differences between the eyes. My concussed brain was not compensating.

One glaring example of how my eyes and brain were not exactly working in sync was how my body responded each day at dismissal time at school. It was always very important to me to be out on the front sidewalk at dismissal to say goodbye to students, hug those who needed hugs, and greet parents who were waiting to take their children home. However, the sight of 600 children leaving the school building and walking down the sidewalk at the same time overwhelmed my concussed brain. My eye movements could not keep up with the children and traffic going by. I would become very dizzy and slightly disoriented. I could not seem to make my eyes move quickly enough or my brain process quickly enough. This was embarrassing for me, and I did not want my staff or students to see me in this weakened condition. I would just look down and walk back inside to my office as if I had some important matter to tend to. Eventually, I rarely was outside at dismissal. This made me feel incompetent and a little like a quitter. But I simply couldn't get my eyes and brain to work in sync enough to stop the dizziness.

At the evaluation session, the concussion team had explained that I would be receiving occupational and physical therapy to help with my remaining symptoms, both balance issues and ocular motor deficits. They also thought it was a good idea to refer me to an optometrist who specialized in concussion recovery. I wasn't exactly seeing double, but I saw shadows of things when I was looking at something that was relatively close to me. In fact, when I sat at a table across from anyone to have a conversation, I would often see more than two eyes on their face and be confused as to which pair of eyes to look at. I had been using a strategy of looking at just one of their eyes. No one ever said that my gaze made them uncomfortable, but my double vision felt awkward for me and I was self-conscious about it. At any rate, I would now be getting help to resolve this issue as well.

So, with these symptoms in mind, the University of Nebraska Medical Center's concussion therapy team devised a personalized plan for recovery. We agreed that I would attend physical and occupational therapy two to three times per week over the summer to clear up the concussion symptoms I was struggling with. At the conclusion of this initial assessment session, the team asked for my input. Specifically, they wanted me to share my personal goals or definition of recovery. I was taken aback by the question. Without missing a beat, I replied simply, "Is it all right if I just say I want my life back?" I couldn't say it without getting choked up as the desperation and mild despair came through. The stunned looks on their faces and the tears in their eyes told me I was in the right place.

At my biweekly OT/PT sessions I was challenged to walk in a straight line, keeping my balance while turning my head from side to side. I would also stand in front of a wall full of sticky notes with the letters of the alphabet on them, scrambled, and then touch the letters in order. Sometimes I had to spell words by touching the letters on the wall. Since the letters were out of order, my eyes had to move around a lot to scan for the letter I was looking for. Spelling words while scanning was excellent exercise for my brain! The sensation of squeezing in my head would increase with these exercises, so the therapists had me sit and take two- to three-minute brain breaks, with no sensory input, between repetitions.

I also did some basic exercises that I had done during my first round of physical therapy. I did eye push-ups by focusing on a pencil that was moved closer and closer and then slowly moved farther away, forcing my eyes to focus at varied distances. I did the same thing with individual beads on a string, focusing on a bead for a count of three and then moving to the next bead farther up the string. At each session I also did an exercise called the "Pinwheel." I would hold a pencil in front of my face and then slowly move it, first like I was making the sign of the cross, then moving it to diagonal corners of an invisible square, thus forming a pinwheel.

After each repetition of all the exercises I was asked to rate my symptoms on a scale of 1 to 10. (My primary symptoms were head pressure, anxiety level, and head pain.) The PT explained that it was okay to take the level of symptoms to a 4, as long as I took a break right away. The predominant and most bothersome symptom that persisted throughout my therapy sessions was the squeezing feeling in my head. Sometimes I called it "the rubber band around my brain" and at other times I called it the "forceps feeling." It felt like someone was reaching into my head with a pair of cold, hard forceps and squeezing my brain whenever it was challenged to do something it did not want to do. I often reported to my OT and PT that my symptoms were a 2 or a 3. But I was downplaying my symptoms—trying to be optimistic, I suppose. In hindsight, and since I have actually felt what 2 or 3 feels like, my symptoms during therapy sessions were at a level of 6 or 7. The good news was that when I sat down, closed my eyes, and rested for a few minutes, the pressure would subside rather quickly. This was a sign that I was creeping out of the rabbit hole.

At one of my summer OT/PT sessions, I happened to run into one of my kindergarten teachers with her teenage daughter. Back in

December during winter break, her daughter had sustained a concussion during a car accident. I remember the teacher coming to me on our first day back from break and talking about her daughter's ordeal. I was worried about her daughter now that I knew females—type A females especially—were particularly vulnerable to post-concussion syndrome. I advised the teacher to let her daughter rest as much as possible and not to let her push herself. The teacher responded by telling me that it was her daughter's junior year of high school and she didn't want to fall behind. As soon as I heard her say that, I knew her daughter was going to be caught in a web of concussion recovery that would not let go easily.

Before running into this young lady at therapy, I had actually told her story to my OT/PT. It was in the context of a discussion about how I had never heard of post-concussion syndrome before experiencing it personally, and now I knew of another female suffering from it. As I described the situation, both of my therapists knew exactly who I was talking about but couldn't say anything due to privacy laws. Later, when I saw this teenager working with my physical therapist and said, "That's her!" my PT and OT both grinned sheepishly and I realized that they had already had contact with her. It was at this point that I began to consider writing this book about my concussion recovery. I felt certain that it was not a simple coincidence that we had the same therapists, with appointments at the same time. With all that I had read about concussions and post-concussion syndrome, there was little to no literature available that focused on females' vulnerability to post-concussion syndrome. Most of the existing information about concussions involved football players or male athletes in general. The seeds for writing about the female experience with concussions in order to help others were planted in the OT/PT office.

As I mentioned earlier, I continued to read and look for signs of hope anywhere I could find them. I had read months earlier that George Clooney had sustained a serious head injury from a fall while filming a movie. His recovery took a full year, and he described it as one of the most difficult years of his life. His head injury had occurred almost ten years before mine. But one day when I was sitting in the waiting room of the OT/PT office thumbing through an issue of People magazine, I saw pictures of George Clooney with his new bride. I remember thinking how happy he looked in those pictures. His eyes glimmered with joy. George

Clooney's recovery from concussion was another beam of hope that I, too, could be symptom-free and happy again one day.

The month of June was going by quickly and I was making great progress. It was enormously helpful to have a break from the everyday stress of my job. A two-day principal summit meeting was scheduled for the end of the month. I remember feeling hopeful and optimistic as I noticed the subtle and not-so-subtle progress I had made. I was able to be in the first all-day meeting, in a large conference room with fluorescent lighting and microphones, without needing to wear my noise-cancelling earbuds. I didn't even have to leave the room to take breaks as a barrage of information was shared. I was not always able to focus and comprehend perfectly, but my brain was tolerating the situation. At one point music was being played as part of the presentation and I actually was able to tolerate that. My experience at this meeting contrasted sharply with January and February's meetings where I was hardly able to be in the meeting room at all.

The school district rarely provided food at our meetings, let alone cocktails. However, at the end of the long day, we were invited to a reception that included free cocktails and hors d'oeuvres. It was a once-in-a-lifetime opportunity that I could not pass up. I enjoyed chatting with my colleagues while sipping white wine—something I would have been unable to do just a few months prior. Until this summit meeting, I hadn't fully realized how much progress I had made. With a few months off work for summer break, maybe I would be able to climb out of the rabbit hole completely. Hope was returning.

But my recovery process during the summer followed the previous "Cha-Cha" pattern of two steps forward and one step back. The week after the principals' summit, I was in my backyard putting some lawn chairs back in place. The backs of the chairs were framed in wrought iron and could fold front or backwards. As I lifted the chair, the back of it fell toward me quickly, knocking me on the head. It was just a slight bump—no big deal, or so I kept telling myself. It hardly even hurt at all. It wasn't a hard enough bump to even leave a bruise. But when I went inside to have dinner with my husband and son, I noticed that they seemed to be talking really loudly. Both my son and husband are actually quiet people who never speak loudly, so I knew it was my perception. Then my husband was telling a story from his workday, and I couldn't comprehend what he was saying. The words were just floating in the air and my brain was unable to absorb them. I was sliding back into the rabbit hole! In a panic, I interrupted my husband. I told Rick and Joe what had happened with the chair and that I knew it sounded crazy, but I thought I might have reconcussed. I got up from the table and went into the living room to lie down on the couch. I wasn't going to move for the whole weekend. I stayed in darkness with no stimuli for two days. I was willing to do anything, no matter how difficult, to escape the grips of my concussion.

When I went to my scheduled OT/PT session the following Tuesday I felt better but still slightly off. I told my physical therapist what had happened, expecting her to tell me that it was just my imagination and a little bump on the head like that could not possibly have made me reconcuss. However, that is not what she said. She nodded in affirmation and understanding. She explained to me that I was more vulnerable to reconcussion than the general population, especially while I still had symptoms of PCS. She shared that one of her patients had reconcussed while riding in a truck on a bumpy road. Getting out of this hole just got more complicated.

In addition to the summer OT/PT sessions, I was seeing an optometrist who specialized in concussion care. She encouraged me to continue doing the eye exercises I was taught at therapy and suggested a few more. She explained that doing word searches would strengthen the scanning skills of my eyes and brain. For the rest of the summer I became a word search guru. I scanned and scanned as though my life depended on it.

Whenever I visited the optometrist, she would hold a pen in front of me and gradually move it closer, asking me to tell her when I began seeing two pens instead of one. I was still seeing double a little too far out, so she suggested I try a slight prism in my reading glasses. My double vision occurred only when I focused on objects that were about three to four feet away from me or closer. The prism glasses were a Godsend. When I used them in place of my reading glasses, with my contacts, my brain was relieved from the need to compensate all the time.

July arrived, and my husband and I took our annual trip to Maine. We often stayed at my aunt and uncle's cabin, which was right on the coast in Owls Head. My sister Deb and her daughter would be joining us this year. There would be no kayaking on the ocean or hiking Mount Battie this summer, but we were looking forward to relaxing near the cool waters of the Atlantic. I had read that flying with a concussion was not a good idea, so we decided to drive. My husband drove all the way from Omaha to Maine—two full days of driving. We put pillows all around me and buckled me into the back seat. There I sat like a padded china doll with noise-cancelling earbuds on to drown out the constant hum of the tires on the road and pillows to soften the jarring of the bumps. No radio. No music. Very little conversation. We were taking every precaution, but I still found riding in the car very draining. I tried lying down so I would not have to process the scenes of the roadside that were whizzing by as we drove down the interstate, but by the time we hit Pennsylvania I was a basket case. Despite the pillows, I was feeling every bump in the road. All I had to do was lie still in the back of the car, yet it was utterly exhausting. My husband Rick was endlessly patient and understanding. By the time we made it to the hotel in Rochelle, New York, I was off balance and severely fatigued all over again. Cha-Cha-Cha.

I felt better the next morning after a good night's sleep. However, we had to get in the car and drive eight more hours until we made it to my family's cabin in Owls Head. There was no turning back, so we continued our journey. We arrived in Owls Head in time to meet my sister and niece at a local restaurant for dinner. We sat outside to minimize the noise. My head pressure was high and I was exhausted, but we had made it to Maine.

Maine had always been my favorite place on earth. Spending time there had always energized and revived me. There was something magical about the cool Atlantic waters, the local artisan cuisine, and relaxing with family. My mom was born and raised in Maine. Although she had passed away more than twenty years prior, I still felt a special connection to her spirit whenever we visited there. In the past, our visits to Maine were a nonstop blur of activity as we made the most of every minute we were there. Running, hiking, kayaking, shopping, and hunting for heart-shaped rocks were all part of the daily agenda. But not this year. I was happy to be there, but I spent most of my time lying on a rock and listening to the soothing sound of the ocean waves. I was exhausted by the drive and spent the entire week resting so I would be able to endure the two-day drive back home. I was, however, able to do a little rock hunting. Strolling along the rocky coast, looking down and scanning for heart-shaped rocks was actually great eye therapy and infinitely more enjoyable than pencil push-ups! The trip was not quite what I had hoped for, but this was my life now and the best I could do.

When we returned home at the end of July it was time for my annual physical exam. I was anxious to update my doctor on the progress I had made and to discuss with her my continued inability to really exercise all-out—to throw myself into heart-pounding, sweat-inducing, muscle-aching exercise. How I missed it! How my body missed it! So when my doctor came into the exam room I began telling her that I was making progress, but it seemed too slow. I told her I was doing a Cha-Cha. Just when I thought I had good momentum going, I would hit a wall. When I re-injured my head with a lawn chair or strained my brain with a long car ride, it took days and sometimes weeks to recover from these setbacks. Like a train that was constantly being derailed, I had to pick myself up and put myself back on the tracks and continue moving toward full recovery. I would often have moments and sometimes days of feeling discouraged. I would allow myself short amounts of time to wallow in self-pity, and then I would remind myself that many people on this planet had it far worse than I did. I would then get back to focusing on what I was able to do, not on what I was still unable to do.

My doctor's response to my description of where I was at in the recovery process was to once again remind me that my age was a factor. She also restated that she wasn't aware of any research evidence that would support my claims that my increased heart rate was related to my increased head pressure. She was not dismissing me; she was just being honest with me. I appreciated my doctor taking the time to discuss my concerns with me. She listened and responded. We had honest, trusting conversations. Not many doctors take the time to really converse with their patients anymore. She reassured me that she would dig deeper into the research, looking for anything about increased PCS symptoms with increased heart rate. In the meantime, she recommended that I stop setting goals, relax, and focus on healing. Yikes! Asking me to stop setting goals was like asking a zebra to stop having stripes. Setting goals was my mode of operation. It was how I had survived so many challenges in my life and how I had become successful at my job. How could I just turn that off?

After the mental storm subsided and I stopped panicking at the thought of not setting goals, I actually felt a moment of relief and peace. The thought of surrendering to what I was experiencing, rather than fighting it at every turn, actually appealed to me. Maybe that was how I should proceed. I wasn't quitting. I wasn't giving up. But I was becoming aware of the value of surrendering to the situation so that I could get out of it. A whole new paradigm! For a brief moment I understood. I surrendered and accepted, and it felt good. However, like walking a tightrope, it was difficult to sustain that balance of acceptance without quitting. I would walk this tightrope daily for the remainder of my recovery process.

My annual physical was not complete yet, however. Since I was aging and a few years into menopause, my doctor thought it would be a good idea for me to undergo a scan to check the density of my bones. The bone scan revealed that my bones were indeed thinning and that I had osteopenia, which is basically pre-osteoporosis. This diagnosis added insult to injury. Osteopenia is not life-threatening, but it is certainly a threat to quality of life. I was well aware that exercise was one of the best ways to keep my bones strong and healthy. So I was faced with a paradox: I needed to exercise, but my head injury prevented me from engaging in strenuous exercise. This realization was a low point for me. Every day I struggled to keep my spirits up and focus on the positive aspects of life. The news about my thinning bones felt like a sucker punch. This latest news increased my sense of urgency to get out of the rabbit hole as quickly as possible.

8

My Swan Song and Walter Payton

The summer months had brought both forward and backward movement in my recovery process. Despite a few minor setbacks like the long drive to Maine and the conk on the head with a lawn chair, I was still improving overall. The summer's physical and occupational therapy sessions were helpful. Unless I was very tired, my balance felt normal. My eyes and brain were working more in sync, although I was still wearing the prism reading glasses for computer use and close-up work. The bad news was that it was time to begin another school year and I was not symptom-free yet. I still could not run or even walk at a rapid pace without increased head pressure. I still needed to be cautious and not overdo. I was still living with one foot on the gas pedal and the other on the brake. My energy levels and stamina were improving but not yet where I wanted them to be. I had thought a two-month break from the stress of my job would surely bring a full recovery, but it had not.

I was acutely aware that I would soon reach the one-year anniversary of my head injury. From what I had read, some people took three months, some six months, and some even a year to be symptom-free after a concussion. So as August began and I was just one month away from the one-year mark, I was optimistic that I would soon be completely free of symptoms. After all, that is what the medical literature said. (I had gone through this same thought process at three months and six months, always clinging to snippets of hope.)

The beginning of the new school year was significant in more ways than one. After this year I would be eligible for early retirement and a decision would need to be made. Our school was beginning a two-year-long major renovation project, and I very much wanted to see it through. Navigating the school through the troubled waters of construction and seeing the completed project would be a satisfying ending to my career with Omaha Public Schools. My swan song.

However, when I returned to school full-time I was immediately hit with reality. The job was stressful enough in a normal year, but this year I had a brand new assistant principal, new guidance counselor, new school nurse, and new secretary. All key positions. The new staff was amazing, talented, and hard-working. However, they were not familiar with the students or rhythm of our school yet, so their presence brought additional pressure for me. Working with new staff members, coupled with beginning the process of renovation planning and my head being in a very fragile healing state, made it impossible for me to be at my best. My head pressure, pain, and fatigue were increasing to flood levels. My condition began backsliding within the first two weeks of the school year. I knew I was not myself, and I was aware that staying at work was jeopardizing my health.

During the previous school year I had put a chair and footstool in my office closet so I could retreat into darkness and silence for brain breaks throughout the day. In the new school year, I did not need to go in the closet to take a break. I was able to sit at my desk, close my eyes, and put my fingers in my ears when I needed a brain break. It was progress, but the fact that I still needed these breaks was disconcerting. So I called the retirement office and made an appointment. The outcome was my decision that this would be my final year as principal at Indian Hill Elementary.

Throughout my healing journey, my greatest cheerleaders had been my family. Their small ways of encouraging me and helping me stay positive were absolute lifelines. My family knew I was contemplating retirement, so my daughter had posted a list of "things Mom can do when she retires" on our kitchen refrigerator. Her list included things like "write, paint, photography, landscape." She also wrote "Get a dog." We'd had a family dog when the children were growing up. But dogs don't live long, and our beloved Maggie passed away just as our youngest was entering college. We had not replaced Maggie for two reasons. First, our lives were very busy. My job entailed very long days and often evenings. My husband's job at Union Pacific was also demanding, and he owned and operated a karate studio on the side. No time for a dog in our lives now. Besides, losing Maggie had been heartbreaking, and my husband and I decided we did not want to go through losing a pet again.

But after I made the decision to retire at the end of the school year, the thought of a four-legged companion became more appealing. I began searching websites and dreaming of getting a dog. Maggie had been a rescue dog, and we favored adopting another dog from a shelter if possible. One Friday evening while I was relaxing and unwinding after a busy school day, my husband decided to visit the Nebraska Humane Society's website. He scanned the available dogs and came across an unkempt, sandy-colored cocker spaniel named "Puck." He showed me Puck's picture and I immediately fell in love. I had to have this dog! The timing was horrible; I still had months to go before retirement. But how often does a cocker spaniel become available for adoption? I asked my daughter to go with me to the Humane Society first thing the next morning to check out Puck.

We arrived at the Humane Society just as it opened and went straight to the kennels of the dogs that were available for adoption. We looked up and down the aisles, but Puck was nowhere in sight. We found a kennel with his name on it, but it was empty. I was sure he had been adopted already. We decided to give up and leave. Just as we were walking out the door, a volunteer asked if he could help us. We explained that we were looking for a specific dog that we had found on the website, but he was not there. The volunteer replied that several of the dogs had been taken to a nearby nursery to show the public and promote adoption. Puck was still available! The volunteer quickly called the staff member at the nursery to tell her to hold Puck because we were coming to get him. It was love at first sight. However, my son was also living with us still, and I felt it was only fair that he have input. The shelter agreed to hold Puck for up to 24 hours so I could bring my husband and son to meet him.

We went back to the Humane Society later that same day. My husband, son, and I waited in a visitation room until Puck was brought in to meet us. The dog wanted absolutely nothing to do with us. He had been playing with a tennis ball, and all he cared about was the ball. He also didn't look like the cute, furry dog we had seen on the website. He had been a tangle of matting when he was brought into the shelter, so they'd had to shave off his fur. He looked pretty odd, but I still wanted him. It was agreed that we would give him a try. However, "Puck" would not do for a name. Our then two-year-old granddaughter was just learning to talk and pronouncing words in interesting ways, as two-year-olds do. For instance, she loved watching "movies" but pronounced the word as "boobies." She would gleefully yell, "I want boobies! I want to see boobies!" As funny as this was, we thought leaving the dog's name "Puck" would have been asking for trouble. We're big Chicago Bears fans, so we decided to rename Puck after our all-time favorite player, Walter Payton.

Like most cocker spaniels, Walter had boundless energy. He was obsessed with playing with tennis balls and needed a walk at least once a day. I would walk him on the trail by Zorinsky Lake often. Soon after getting Walter I took him for a walk and was feeling strong that day. I was able to walk at a faster pace than usual. Up ahead was a fellow walker, and I was pretty sure my dog and I would be able to pass him. It was exciting to realize that I could actually walk fast enough, with minimal head symptoms, to pass someone on the trail! (This man was probably in his late sixties or early seventies, but I didn't care about that detail. I just cared that I was able to pass someone.) As we walked briskly past this gentleman, he jokingly commented that he would now have to go home and tell his wife he had been passed on the trail by a woman and her dog. I retorted, "Tell your wife you were passed by the Flash and Walter Payton!"

My new companion would quickly become my therapy dog. Walter took my mind off my troubles and kept me moving. Like so many aspects of my life at the time, Walter would turn out to be a mixed blessing. It was just part of the Cha-Cha.

I had to wait until the end of September to sign the official retirement papers. It wasn't easy to do so. I had given eighteen years of my life to the Omaha Public Schools. The majority of my career had been spent serving our society's most marginalized students. I was and still am a strong believer in the power of education. High-quality public education is the hallmark of our democracy. More importantly, it is the only way out of poverty. I would often preach to my teachers that we were doing far more than teaching reading, writing, and arithmetic. We were breaking the poverty cycle. Most of the schools I served had high proportions of immigrant, migrant, and refugee students. I cherished working with these students and their families. Outside of caring for my own family, helping these families was my purpose in life. I was doing what the Universe had called me to do, and I felt like I was making a positive difference. So signing the retirement papers felt as if I was letting go of my purpose in life. I knew I did not have a choice, because my health depended on retiring at this point. And since the Universe had never let me down before and had always showed me the way, I just had to take a leap of faith that I would figure out my new purpose when the time was right.

Now that the retirement decision had been made, I was ready to focus on finishing my final year on a positive note. I had always given at least 100% to my job, but my new 100% was only about 75% of what I used to be able to do. My energy and stamina were still weak. I still struggled with basics like being outside at the end of the school day to help supervise dismissal. By the end of the day, I was so exhausted that I didn't have the stamina to stand on the sidewalk for 10 to 15 minutes. I was still having ocular motor issues, and watching the children walk past me down the hill would make me feel very dizzy and light-headed. I don't know why this continued to embarrass me, but it did. By this time, all the staff and families had heard about my head injury and were aware that I had not fully recovered. Call it ego, pride, or whatever, but I did not want my staff or students to see me as this weakened version of myself. I liked being viewed as strong—as The Flash, a superhero. But because I was only functioning cognitively and physically at about 75%, I found myself hunkered down in my office too much of the time. I preferred to be in the classrooms observing teachers, greeting students in the hallways, leading the charge.

In an effort to survive the remainder of my final year as principal, I decided to get strategic. I did not want to be remembered as the principal who hit her head and ended her career unable to lead. I had a finite amount of energy to use each day, so I made a conscious choice to use it all for Indian Hill. I would table my physical and occupational therapy exercises and anything else that stole my limited energy and reserve it solely for my staff and students. I told only two staff members about my retirement and asked them to keep it confidential until January. I hated long good-byes.

My new assistant principal was quite talented, and staff and students loved him from the beginning. I shared with him my intention to retire and asked him if he wanted to prepare to take my place. I realized that I wouldn't be able to choose the person who would replace me, but I had a strong desire to ensure that the school would be left in capable hands. After he had consulted his wife, he decided to apply to be the new principal. During the rest of the school year he and I worked together to prepare him and the instructional leadership team (math coach, reading coach, instructional facilitator) to take over the reins.

I had always held weekly leadership team meetings, usually on Mondays. At these meetings we planned and fine-tuned professional development for the staff, discussed how to meet the needs of struggling students, and sifted through student data. During my final year I decided to hold a "Leadership Boot Camp" at the first meeting of each month. At the boot camp sessions we set aside our regular agenda and focused specifically on growing as leaders. I would share relevant professional articles or some inspiring passage and then we would discuss. My assistant principal agreed to take over leading the boot camp sessions in January as part of his preparation for the principal's role. This would provide practice for him and one less thing for me to spend my limited energy on.

In addition to stepping up my efforts to prepare leadership for my absence, I planned ways to spend more time with my students. I knew how much I was going to miss them. Our wonderful librarian had a group of intermediate students who participated in a book club, reading young adult literature. It had become super cool to be part of this group, "The Golden Sower Book Club." Score! Just what we were aiming for, making reading cool for inner-city kids. But a number of the students who joined the club did not have the reading skills to handle some of the more difficult texts. To help them save face and to give me more time with them, I created a Read with the Principal group.

The students had a mix of reading abilities, and I purposely included students we knew would struggle. We met weekly before school to read together and talk about the text. I would provide donuts to entice the kids to arrive early. I loved discussing the text with them and hearing them share their thoughts and ideas. This meant extra reading for me, and it was difficult. But I was reserving my cognitive and physical energy for activities like these. I could almost see the sand in the hourglass slipping down quickly, and I urgently needed to soak up as much time with my students as I could manage before leaving.

Supervising the cafeteria at lunchtime continued to be a struggle for me. My filter was better but still not fixed yet. When fourteen tables of students had several conversations occurring at once, I still struggled with filtering it all out. I heard everything at once, and the pressure in my head increased as soon as I entered the cafeteria. It was hard to stay there for more than a few minutes, so I found another way to connect with my kids at lunchtime. I had groups of students, usually troubled souls but not always, who requested to have lunch with me. So two or three times a week I ate lunch with small groups of students in my office. I liked the fact that students wanted to spend time with me, and I also was glad that my kids understood that being in the principal's office wasn't always a bad thing.

As I mentioned earlier, the school was beginning to plan for a two-year renovation project. As always we had a limited budget, so not everything on our wish list was possible. The majority of the renovation funds would be used to replace the old boiler system that heated the building. After the new furnace had been installed, there would be no more "bang-clank-bang" in the classrooms whenever the heat kicked on! We were also slated to get central air conditioning. The building was older than I was, and we had survived the warmest days by relying on window air conditioning units in the classrooms. But these window units were not very efficient. I was called to classrooms on more than one occasion to handle a rebellious window unit that had decided to spit out ice pellets. The teachers and I joked about getting pelted with ice, but it wasn't really funny. My students already had to deal with enough adversity in their lives. They deserved a school building that would provide shelter from life's storms.

So basic structural needs soaked up the majority of the renovation budget. That left nothing to update the front of the building. Our school was the safe haven, the lighthouse, in a challenging neighborhood. It was very important to me that it look like the safe haven that it was. I was discouraged that there wasn't any money in the budget to update the exterior of this 1950s relic. Then I received an email from a dear friend who was the coordinator of our ESL department (English as a Second Language). A community organization called Justice for Our Neighbors had received a grant to paint a mural of an immigrant Mexican woman, and they were looking for a building to put the painting on. The organization and the local artist, Watie White, wanted to know if Indian Hill would be interested in a mural. This was excellent news! It would make the front of the school building more welcoming and cost the school nothing. I was ecstatic, both for my school and for myself. I would be leaving Indian Hill on a high note, just as I had hoped.

Watie came to the school and visited with me in person about the project. I showed him the front brick wall of the school that I thought would be perfect for the mural. When he saw how large the space was, he decided to expand the project and add two more pictures. He asked if he could include two immigrant students from our school.

What a wonderful idea! I could not have been more thrilled for the Indian Hill community. After speaking with teachers, we chose a male student from Somalia and a female student from Togo. The artist's process included interviewing the students and then painting some of their own words inside the picture of them on the mural. The goal was to emphasize our common humanity.

And to make the experience even more personalized, Watie invited students to help paint the mural. We had a big celebration the day the students began painting. We had music from a local Mariachi Band, treats from the International Bakery on 24th Street, and songs from our own student chorus. The executive director of Justice for Our Neighbors attended, along with our representatives in the state legislature and U.S. Congress. The event was a big deal, and I could barely take it all in. The celebration was held in the afternoon, when my brain energy was usually depleting the fastest. It was also warm for an October day. These little details—timing, temperature—matter when your brain is concussed. A normal brain can accommodate slight discomforts like heat and fatigue, but my concussed brain still was working on regaining its ability to function fully under less-than-perfect conditions. I managed to survive the event, but it drained my already low battery down to zero.

This joyous occasion would be overshadowed by fear and gun violence just weeks later. Our school's first round of parent-teacher conferences took place annually in mid-October. We held ours during one full day and two evenings in order to provide flexibility for our parents' myriad working schedules. It was an extra-long day for our teachers and other staff members: a full school day with students and then four hours of conferences. Parent-teacher conference days had exhausted me under normal circumstances, and I knew that my recovering brain would increase my fatigue. I easily could have gone home and told my staff my head couldn't handle the long day. But because this was my final year, I chose to stick it out. I did take many brain breaks and spent a good portion of the evening in my dark office, trying to get the low-battery light in my brain to stop glowing.

I usually tried to be one of the last ones out of the building during parent-teacher conference time. I had always felt that if a teacher or translator was still present in the building, I needed to be there, too. Our night custodians were very helpful, but as the building leader I felt compelled to be there until the end. That evening, as I locked my office and saw that the majority of staff had left, I began to exit the building and walk toward my car, which was parked about a block down the street from the main entrance. I had never felt scared in my school's neighborhood before—not ever. I freely walked in the projects doing home visits when I needed to. Everyone knew me and as unfair as it was, as a white woman I felt immune from the neighborhood violence that sometimes broke out. But this evening was different. It was dark, I was tired, and as soon as I stepped onto the sidewalk the hair went up on the back of my neck. Something felt wrong. I noticed a tall black man walking up the sidewalk toward school. I did not recognize him and it just didn't feel right. I told myself that it was wrong to make assumptions just because he was black, and I continued walking toward my car. Just as I was crossing the street, a car came barreling around the corner. The engine had no muffler and was very loud. I had to hurry to get out of the middle of the street. That's when time slowed way down, like you see in the movies. The car squealed to a stop as someone inside fired off a round of about five gunshots at the tall black man, who by this time was about five yards from me. I remember hearing my night custodian, who was out escorting a final teacher to her car, yell, "Get down, get down!" I just stood there, stunned. I remember thinking, "Oh, this is what a drive-by shooting looks like." It was all happening in slow motion and unreal to me. I was dazed. The car peeled off and turned the corner at the top of our street. I snapped out of my daze, put my satchel down and ran over to the spot where I expected to find a dead body. I was firing off all kinds of expletives and yelling, "Where's the guy who got shot? Where's the guy who got shot?" My cell phone was in my hand, but I couldn't think clearly enough to dial 911. My hands were shaking, and my head pain and pressure soared to unusually high levels. I wasn't focused on my head symptoms, however—I wanted to know where the injured guy was. Surely he would need medical assistance. My custodian told me he had seen the man run through our school parking lot.

Although it seemed like an eternity passed while we waited, several police cruisers arrived within minutes. They taped off the area and began searching for bullet casings. They discovered that the shooter had used a starter gun filled with blanks. The young man was able to run away because he hadn't been shot. The police said that the shooter was probably just trying to scare him.

I think the shooter didn't realize he had blanks in his gun; he definitely was hunting this young man and the young man knew it.

Nothing more came of the shooting. There was no victim and no blood. The police didn't find the target or the shooter. But the event left a scar on my staff. I knew rumors would fly, so I quickly sent out a message to all staff describing the incident and listing the facts. I scheduled a staff meeting first thing the next morning so teachers could ask questions and vent their fears. There were no students in the building the following day due to parent-teacher conferences, so I was able to focus on soothing the staff's anxieties about the shooting. This scenario would of course have been difficult for anyone, but my concussed brain and its low tolerance for stress quadrupled the complexity of the situation. Concussed brains do not handle emotions well. So when I stood up to speak to the staff and calm their anxieties, I began to cry like a baby. I could not believe my head couldn't hold it together just for this one meeting. I wanted to stay composed in front of the staff, but my brain wasn't able to handle the intense emotions I was feeling. I told the staff that I appreciated all their hard work and that the last thing they needed on top of all their other challenges was to be afraid at work. I asked them what they needed to feel safe, as we had one more day and evening of parent-teacher conferences to get through. They requested a visible police presence as well as personal escorts by male staff to their cars after conferences. I promised them I would ensure that they had whatever they needed to be safe and feel safe.

I was so proud of my staff. They didn't just think of themselves and the trauma of the shooting. They talked about their realization that the fear they felt was something that many of our students lived with on a daily basis. They felt a renewed sense of appreciation for the resilience of our students and their families and our mission as a school. When all was said and done and the dust had settled, I looked toward the sky and said to the Universe, "Really! I already signed the retirement papers. I got the message! I don't need any more signs, thank you very much!"

9

The Elephant Has Landed On My Head Again

As the school year continued, I maintained my equilibrium as best I could. After the shooting I had several nights of reliving the experience. I would close my eyes to try to sleep and then I would see the spark from the gun again. I would hear five gunshots, like firecrackers going off. I would see the little flame at the opening of the gun. And then I would hear the car peel off. Anytime I heard a car with a loud muffler, my heart would pound and my head pressure would rise. This all seemed like normal processing of a traumatic event. Old me would have run the stress off, but that was no longer an option. At this point, I was only capable of walking about a half mile. I did what I could. Each morning before I went to work, Walter Payton and I would go for a walk under the early morning starry sky. He needed the exercise, and I needed the stress relief. The walk in the cool air was meditative for me. Although walking helped control my stress levels to some extent, it was not as effective as a good, heart-pounding run. Winter break was coming soon, and I was looking forward to having two full weeks to focus on resting, putting the shooting behind me, and fully recharging my battery.

Christmas had always been a special time at our house. We traditionally celebrated on Christmas Eve with our three adult children and two granddaughters. Then the day after Christmas we would all caravan to Wisconsin to spend a week with my sister and her family. On Christmas Eve we woke to a record-breaking snowfall. It was wonderful—the kind of wet snow that coats the tree branches and blankets everything with simple beauty. Our three children and two grandchildren would be gathering at our house at 9:00 for a pancake breakfast and then opening gifts. Walter Payton could get pretty excited around our grandkids, so we thought we should take him for a short walk prior to their arrival. That way he might be a little less energetic during the festivities.

The snow under our feet was not slick at all. In fact, it was crunchy and my husband mentioned that it was the perfect snow for running. I used to love to run in the snow because it was so peaceful. We continued walking toward the park near our house. We walked along, aiming toward the path that led to the woods of Zorinsky Lake. I still couldn't walk far, so we were planning to turn around when we reached the path. But just as we stepped onto the unplowed sidewalk, our feet flew out from under us. Under the beautiful layer of snow was a thick sheet of ice. I landed mostly on my left butt cheek and caught myself with my left arm. I did not hit my head on the pavement. But my feet had flown out from underneath me, and I had gone up in the air and landed hard. The jarring was sharp. My husband asked if I was okay and I replied, "I don't know." I had that weird feeling that had grown all too familiar. We returned home and I immediately got into bed and became completely still. I was hoping to ward off what I knew was coming.

I did not want to cancel our holiday festivities, so the kids arrived as planned. Of course everyone was excited; it was Christmas! But their voices seemed exceptionally loud. I did not tell my family how bad I was feeling because I did not want to ruin their holiday. My head injury had taken up enough of our family's time and attention. I wasn't going to let it steal the show again.

We opened gifts, ate all day, played all day, and just enjoyed spending time together. I tried to move minimally and take a slow pace, but it was a long day. My husband is the cook in our family, so he was doing all the cooking anyway. I usually do the cleanup, but I wasn't able to help this time. We had planned to attend the Christmas Eve service at the First Unitarian Church, but it had been cancelled due to the heavy snowfall. I was in bed by seven that night, exhausted. I couldn't deny it any longer: the elephant had landed on my head again.

I woke up Christmas morning and the light from the morning sun reflecting off the layers of new snow was immensely bright. Every sound was much too loud. I had a pulsing, crushing headache. My head felt like it was back in a vise that someone was cranking tight. I had hoped that going to bed early and getting a good night's sleep would allow me to wake up and be fine. But I knew I had reconcussed. Is that what you call it when you haven't even healed from the first concussion? Or is it a new concussion on top of the old one? I'm not sure how to describe it. All I know is that the wind had been taken out of my already flailing sails. Would I have the resolve to rest and do what was needed in order to recover? That may sound simple, but it's not. Concussion recovery takes an enormous amount of cognitive and emotional energy. It is an indescribable fatigue. Discouragement washed over me like a tidal wave. I had been struggling for over a year with keeping my spirits up and trying to do the right thing for my brain's healing process. But now here I was again, sucked down deeper into the rabbit hole. As I was lying on the couch on Christmas morning with my eyes covered to keep out the bright light, I prayed that I would not have to go through this again: "Please don't make me. Please don't make me."

My son stopped by to pick up something one of the girls had left at our house the day before. They were on their way to Wisconsin. I told him not to worry about me, because I would rest all day and be fine by morning. We would just delay our trip one day.

I woke up the day after we were supposed to arrive at my sister's house and called to let her know that I simply couldn't make the trip this year. I had spent every Christmas of my entire life with Debbie, my sister and best friend. So not being able to travel to Wisconsin was a huge morale blow that made it even more difficult to keep my spirits up.

I couldn't even cry because it would have made my head hurt too much. Lying perfectly still in our quiet house, I felt sorry for myself. But as it had in the past, something rose up deep from within me: a voice that told me not to get lost in my self-pity; I would be okay. I got the notion to send my husband to the bookstore. A few weeks earlier I had listened to an NPR interview with the author of a book about concussion recovery, and I had intended to get a copy of the book. Now I had the time to read it. Rick's trek to Barnes and Noble was a success. He came home with *The Ghost in My Brain: How a Concussion Stole My Life and How the New Science of Brain Plasticity Helped Me Get It Back* by Clark Elliott.

The title of the book appealed to me because it mentioned "brain plasticity." I also was attracted to the part about getting one's life back. Throughout my healing process I had been aware that not everyone makes it back to 100%. The fear of not healing completely was constantly with me. But something in the wording of the title made me think I had a chance. As I turned to the dedication page at the beginning of the book, tears flowed as I read the following words: "To the millions who suffer head injuries each year. There is hope." Powerful, simple words.

I had received a journal from my son and his wife for Christmas. The front cover was personalized with a collage of photos of my family.

It was titled "Sharon Royers' Writing Journal." I opened it and began taking notes as I read Clark Elliott's book. I felt fortunate that I could read. I knew that many people with concussions could not focus to read for a long time. When I wore my prism reading glasses to help my eyes work together, I could read, think, record. The first thoughts I wrote were "I can't keep living like this. I want my life back."

I couldn't believe what I was reading. I related to the author's story on so many levels. I began to record page numbers from the book along with my thoughts and feelings regarding his story. It felt so good to have someone put into words so articulately what I had been experiencing. It is so easy to feel alone, as if you are the only person stuck in concussion recovery. Like a balm on a wound, just reading Elliott's words had a healing effect on me.

Here are a few excerpts from the notes I made in my journal as I read *The Ghost in My Head*:

> ***p. 6*** *Author describes his sheer exhaustion, but feeling like he had no choice. He loved his work and had a sense of obligation. I relate to this. I could not just take time off and heal. Indian Hill was not going to run itself!*

p. 7 *Author describes needing a "completely different kind of nothing." I would go in my dark closet at work, close my ears and eyes and try for absolute* <u>*nothingness*</u>*! It was the only way to regain enough strength to get through the day.*

p. 8 *Author talks about being very tired. I relate! It is not emotional; it is very physical.*

p. 31 *Used to be an excellent multi-tasker, but could now just do (comprehend) one thing at a time.*

p. 34 *Author wishes doctors would have given a more precise description of what a concussion is. I don't blame my doctor, but I do wish I had been warned about post-concussion syndrome specifically.*

pp. 37–38 *Author describes using words and phrases incorrectly, like "over-serving" instead of "observing." This would happen to me, too. And when it did, I knew I was not using the right word, but I didn't seem to have a pathway to get to the right one.*

pp. 41–42 *Describes his emergency room experience—very painful! I agree! Emergency room doctors and nurses seem to be trained in identifying concussion, but need to be trained* *in how to communicate to the concussed patient HOW to care for the concussion. To start with, verbal instructions don't work for a concussed person! We only comprehend about half of what you say because we cannot process fast enough. Then what we did comprehend, we don't remember later!*

p. 47 *"In short, at the time, the standard neurologists' response to concussion was to give me an exam designed for dementia, and, my having passed that, and a simple set of reflex tests, send me home." Yep! I remember the dementia questions… this method of exam misses the mark!*

I continued reading and journaling, gobbling up the book as if my life depended on it. Then I read a passage that helped put my mindset back on the right track. On page 195 Elliott described an epiphany he had experienced after struggling for two years with his concussion symptoms:

In that moment, I just let go. I accepted that life as I had known it was over. But this explicitly did not mean that I was giving up. In fact, in a baroque way it was the opposite of giving up. Rather it was a giving in—a complete reorganization of how I felt about my time on earth.

Those words "giving in, not giving up" clicked with me. I realized that I needed to surrender to what was while simultaneously working my way out of the rabbit hole. This is absolutely the key to full healing. Surrender, but don't give up!

In his book, Clark Elliott said that it took him eight years to get his life back. I was only on year two. His book was a vital turning point for me. Mindset is everything when your brain has been injured. And of course, because it is the brain—the mind—that is broken, it is even harder to maintain a positive, healthy mindset. Hearing about and reading about other survivors' stories was exactly what I needed and a necessary piece of the healing puzzle.

I continued to be still, sleep a lot, and generally rest for the remainder of that winter break. No TV, no phone, no computers. I continued popping fish oil capsules until I could almost feel the gills growing out of the sides of my neck! It all helped; I felt myself recovering much more quickly this time. I had to be functional by January 4, the day my staff and I would return to school.

Fortunately, the first day back from break was a teacher work day, with no students. Normally we did not have staff meetings on teacher work days, but I asked my staff to meet me in the library at the start of the day for a quick announcement. I planned to let them know I would be retiring at the end of the school year. Human Resources would begin its search for a replacement soon, so I had to tell my staff before they found out through the grapevine. I had prepared just days before by writing a speech. I was afraid I would get in front of my nearly 50 teachers and forget how to say what I wanted to say. Like a scratched record, sometimes my brain worked smoothly without a catch, but sometimes it would get stuck and not be able to find a word I was trying to speak. I didn't want this to happen in front of everyone, so I wrote down exactly what I wanted to say. I had made the conscious decision to stay unemotional, stay professional. I wasn't going to make it about me. I wanted it to be about them. What was I thinking? I couldn't even get the first sentence out without breaking down and crying.

I began with "Seven years ago we started our ....sob...sob...oh, shit!" My expletive added comic relief to a tense and emotional moment. Teachers laughed and then cried as I gathered myself together and finished my prepared speech:

> *Seven years ago we started our good-to-great journey together. We set out to make*

Indian Hill a model urban school. We have achieved this goal together. We paved the way for all the other OPS Title I schools and created a "Restructure Plan" that was second to none. I have felt enormously privileged to work with such a talented and dedicated staff. This, however, is my final year. I am retiring at the end of this school year. I have mixed emotions about retiring, but my head injury cinched the decision. I had hoped to at least stay until construction was complete. I thought it would be amazing to leave with a completely remodeled building. Now I feel a bit like Moses, leading my people to the promised land of no banging boilers and no spitting window air conditioners, but unable to complete the journey with you. … I want you all to know that I actually believe in our cheesy phrase: 'Finish Strong!' I am committed to working my ass off and doing the best I can to leave Indian Hill poised to continue its journey as a model urban school. It is too early to be sad. Let's roll up our sleeves and make this final semester together the most amazing yet!

And with those words I began my final semester as principal of Indian Hill Elementary.

10

Finishing Strong!

Each Monday morning I would go on our school's intranet television with words of inspiration for the students and staff. We would conclude by reciting our "Finish Strong" pledge together: "Indian Hill Bears START strong, STAY strong, and FINISH strong!" I would flex my biceps as I said the words, trying to really ham it up so the kids would remember. My kindergarten and first-grade students seemed to appreciate this the most. They would often stop me in the hallway, outside on the sidewalk, or in the lunchroom and show me their muscles while reciting our pledge. But now this phrase, this pledge, took on a whole new meaning for me personally.

As January turned into February, I was acutely aware that this would be my final semester as principal and educator with the Omaha Public

Schools. Retirement is a very emotional time for most people, especially if you love what you do. I would find myself feeling weepy often in the final months of the school year. This was part head injury, part menopause, and part me. The feelings were legitimate and understandable. But my head injury's role was that once I started to feel any emotion strongly, it became a runaway train and I wasn't able to reel it in very easily. Well aware of this, I tried to remain guarded and stoic. But it wasn't easy.

Like a parent who is helping a grown child leave the nest, I put all my energy into making sure Indian Hill Elementary would continue on a course of excellence. I spent a lot of time with my assistant principal, hoping that he would follow in my footsteps as the next leader of the school. He had plenty of experience in his own right, but nothing prepares you to lead a school until you do it. He was wonderfully open to my suggestions, coaching, and slight mania about having everything prepared for my departure.

My head was holding its own. I was driving myself to and from school daily. I could manage to get through a full school day as long as I took a few brain breaks. These breaks involved turning my computer screen off, sitting still in my office chair, and just breathing. I would close my eyes, and if my head pressure was rising I would cover my eyes and ears to minimize any stimulation. I knew I was improving, however, because I rarely needed to cover my eyes and ears anymore. And I didn't need to hunker down in my closet!

Although I recognized that my stamina was improving at work, I was still unable to do any exercise that was more vigorous than a brisk walk. The previous year I had been unable to walk very far or very fast, so this was progress. But I knew something still wasn't right. Three major symptoms still plagued me: (1) My head would not tolerate exercise or stress of any kind that brought my heart rate above 95, and my heart seemed to reach that rate much too quickly. (2) My head felt like a car engine that was idling too high. There was a constant hum of anxiety. I couldn't seem to calm down my mind or my neuro-insides. This anxiety was especially troublesome as I tried to fall asleep after a long day at work. My brain engine wanted to continue to idle instead of settling down. (3) Since my head injury I had lost my sensation of needing to urinate. When my bladder was full, my head pressure would rise and I would get a loud hum in my head. Sometimes I would get this sensation and forget why and what I needed to do.

I never had any accidents, but out of an abundance of caution I would empty my bladder nearly every hour. Just one more logistical issue to manage!

In April I made a follow-up appointment with my family physician to update her on my progress. I described my three primary concerns that were most troublesome, although they were not my only symptoms. My light/sound sensitivity and balance issues had cleared up for the most part, yet these symptoms returned when I became tired or pushed myself too hard. She listened to me describe my inability to exercise for the third time in over a year. Only this time she didn't proclaim that there wasn't any research to back up the connection between my rapid heart rate and head squeezing. She told me she had another concussion patient who was describing exactly the same symptoms as mine. I greatly appreciated my doctor's candor and honesty. She said she would search further into the medical literature and send information to me via email as soon as she found something.

Within just a few days, my doctor emailed an article to me entitled "Physiologic Post Concussion Disorder" (found on Brainline.org). The article describes a fictitious male athlete who sustained a concussion and months later was still unable to tolerate exercise that increased his heart rate. Wow!

The answer to my prayers! I was not crazy after all. I was not the only one who felt head squeezing when I tried to exercise or anything made my heart rate increase. The article actually described the sensation as a rubber band tightening. Exactly how it felt! And the article had answers.

I felt validated and hopeful that I would actually recover and be able to run again. I desperately missed sweating, heart-pounding, all-out exertion. I was so tired of living with my brakes on!

In response to this new information, my doctor prescribed blood pressure medication for me. Prior to my head injury I tended to have low blood pressure. My blood pressure was not technically high. However, since my concussion, my resting pressure tended to be about 132 over 80. That was very high for me since I was used to it being closer to 120 over 60s. The elevated blood pressure explained why I felt like my engine was idling too high all the time.

I began taking 25 mg of Metoprolol Succinate ER daily. In addition, my lower back was bothering me again, so my doctor prescribed an anti-inflammatory medication. I'd had lower back issues since I was in my late twenties, but I had controlled the pain by running and staying reasonably fit. A year and a half of not being able to exercise had caught up with me. My back needed me to move, but my head needed me not to move. It was a paradox! But as soon as I started taking these medications I felt the engine in my brain quiet and the constant pressure in my head subside. I felt a significant improvement. I began trying to do a light jog on my morning walks and found that I could do it with minimal increase in head pressure. I was on my way!

To clarify, the medications did not eliminate my symptoms, but they definitely lessened them and helped me to function better. Although I took the anti-inflammatory for my back, it seemed to be helping my head as well. My stamina for getting through the stressful days had improved, and I was adding light jogging on my two-mile walks. I could only jog about 100 yards before my head pressure rose too high, but it was progress! I would walk about a quarter mile, jog what I could, then walk another quarter mile, then jog what I could. This was my pattern. After exercising I would need to drink a big glass of water and then sit perfectly still with my eyes and ears covered for a good 10 to 15 minutes in order to give my brain a chance to recover. Although I was making progress, it was slow… snail's pace slow. To keep from getting frustrated, I reminded myself that I was able to walk at a decent pace and distance only after walking slowly for five minutes a day, then building from there very cautiously and gradually. I would have to invoke this strategy again to regain my ability to run, but I was making progress.

It was such a relief to be feeling better, especially since I still had four weeks of school to get through. The final weeks of any school year are intense, but this year being my last made it doubly so. The renovations for the school building had actually begun in April. Since we weren't completely tearing down the building, we did not have a groundbreaking ceremony per se. However, we did want to do something to commemorate the start of the school's remodel. I coordinated a "Renovation Celebration" to be held on May 5, Cinco de Mayo. We had a live mariachi band play music as parents, central office staff, and our city councilman arrived. CEOs from the architect team and construction company attended as well. The entire school body was on the front lawn, poised to celebrate this new beginning. The students sang a song in unison, and ceremonial shovels were used to symbolically throw dirt.

I was well aware that this might be my last opportunity to address the entire student body and staff in one setting. I wanted them all to know how much I loved them and how much I would miss them. But this was not the time to do that. And once again, I realized this was not about me. This was about them, so I prepared the following words to conclude the ceremony: (Again, I wrote out verbatim what I wanted to say for fear that I would forget what I wanted to say and be embarrassed in front of everyone.)

> *Indian Hill Students, Staff, and Community: I would like to leave you with two important thoughts. First, on this 5th day of May, or Cinco de Mayo, I would like to share one of my favorite quotes by Cesar Chavez, a Mexican-American who helped lead the cause for social justice in our country. He said, "Preservation of one's own culture does not require contempt or disrespect for other cultures." During this political climate of negativity and hateful words, I thought it important that we be reminded that the United States of America is big enough and great enough for all cultures! Here at Indian Hill we believe there is NO PLACE FOR HATE and that KINDNESS MATTERS. Secondly and lastly, students, I thought this would be a good opportunity to learn some*

new vocabulary. Since this is a "renovation celebration," I Googled the word "Renovation" to look for words to help me explain what it means, and this is what I found: "Restore (something old, especially a building) to a good state of repair. Modernize. Refurbish. Revamp. Recondition." Here are my two favorites: "Refresh and Reinvigorate." May this renovation project not only refresh and reinvigorate the building, but also your spirits and your resolve to continue to make Indian Hill the best school it can be.

The ceremony concluded and teachers corralled their students back to the classrooms. I shook hands with the various guests in attendance and received a number of compliments. I drank it in. Then I quietly retreated to my office chair and cried. When I was alone, I could let the runaway train go.

My wonderful staff planned a retirement party for me. I had an inkling that it would involve a special video segment. One of our students with autism had stopped me in the hallway several times to say, "Mrs. Royers, I hope you like the movie we made for you! I hope you like the movie!" It was very sweet and a great prelude.

As the retirement party neared, I was worried once again that the emotional runaway train would get the better of me. But to my surprise and delight, I was not sad at the party. I was filled with joy and appreciation for my staff and past staff members who had come back to wish me well. As my student had hinted, a movie had been prepared for me. Each grade level had created a special segment to bid me a fond farewell. There were funny songs, student testimonials, and sweet words, all peppered with lots of love and humor. I felt every bit of it and drank it in. After nearly 20 years with the Omaha Public Schools, my passion, time, and energy had all boiled down to this wonderful moment of celebration. The staff was aware that I was a huge Chicago Bears fan but had never seen a game in person, and they took up a collection and bought two tickets so Rick and I could attend an October game. The gift was so special, not just because I love the Bears but because I felt in that moment that my staff knew me. That's always a good feeling! Although I had been through hell and back with my concussion recovery, I was still able to feel like the luckiest person in the world. I felt joyful. I felt appreciated. I felt loved. It doesn't get better than that!

11

A Conversation with the Cabinet Door

My best friend and dear sister, Debbie, was also planning to retire at the end of the school year. She was a passionate and dedicated special education teacher in Wisconsin. Deb worked primarily with students who had behavior disorders. Her job, too, was enormously stressful. You might think working with challenging children was the source of her stress, but it wasn't. The politics of education and unsupportive administrators were her stress points. So after 20 years of teaching, she had decided to retire.

Throughout our lives we had experienced a mystical connection. My aunt called us Irish twins because we were so close in age, born just 18 months apart. In high school we were on the same sports teams. In college we were roommates.

We were maids of honor in each other's weddings. And as we became mothers, we managed to become pregnant at precisely the same time. Both of Deb's children were born within two weeks of my youngest two. We could finish each other's sentences and often phoned each other just when the other was about to call. We were connected in a spiritual, mystical way. Perhaps it was surviving our chaotic childhood together that had forged our strong bond. Whatever the reason, here we were again at a significant point in our lives, going through the same transition together.

I wanted to give my sister a special retirement gift—something memorable that would help us transition out of school life and into retirement. I thought a spa-like retreat together would be just the thing. But when I did an Internet search for information, all the nice spas were simply too far away. My head was not well enough for long-distance travel. Deb's husband was planning to host a joint retirement party for us in Oconomowoc that June. It was really Deb's party and they were very generous to include me. Since I would be in Wisconsin in June for the party, I decided to look for spa retreats within driving distance of Deb's house.

I spent weeks researching and in all of my Internet searches, the Christine Center in Willard, Wisconsin, kept popping up. I resisted it because I was looking for a pampering spa experience for both of us, not a spiritual awakening. But after about the fifth time that the center popped up on my computer screen, I decided to take a closer look. I started with the dates we would be available, just after the retirement bash my brother-in-law was throwing. The Christine Center was offering a four-day retreat entitled "The Inner Life of Stories: Writing as Deep Listening" that aligned perfectly with the dates I was searching for. A writers' workshop wasn't exactly a pampering spa, but the description of the center and this particular retreat intrigued me. So I explored further. I had decided that I wanted to write a book about my concussion experience. Aside from journaling, I really had no idea how to start. So maybe this experience would be beneficial after all. Besides, I thought, the workshop promised a lot of time alone to write. If we didn't write and just relaxed in the beautiful wooded setting, who would know?

I emailed the workshop leader and author, Elizabeth Andrew, to be sure we wouldn't be getting in over our heads. I explained to her that Deb and I were not authors or even really writers, but that we were looking for a relaxing experience to jump start our retired lives. Elizabeth said we could attend her workshop, but we would need to bring some of our writing with us to share in group sessions and we would need to be willing to write.

Before making the reservation for us, I called my sister and described what I was trying to give her as a retirement gift. Since this involved a bit more of a commitment than I had originally intended, I thought it best to get Deb's permission before I committed us to this thing. She did not hesitate. Although this was turning more into a retirement gift to myself, Deb was willing to go along with me. She would be my chauffeur, my roommate, my comic relief, and my sounding board for this retreat.

The Christine Center turned out to be exactly what I needed! It was serene, peaceful and beautiful. The retreat center had been founded by Franciscan Sisters on 251 wooded acres. We stayed in the main building, which had indoor plumbing and air conditioning but no televisions, phones, or loud noises. My brain benefited from four straight days of healthful eating and lots of quiet time. Other than our short workshop sessions, the only sounds we heard were from the chirping birds fluttering around the many bird feeders or the toads croaking near the ponds. I hadn't intended for the retreat to be therapeutic for my brain, but it was.

Our writers' workshop session began with introductions. We each described briefly what and why we were writing. We went around the circle of about twelve of us, each sharing a bit of our souls with total strangers. I shared that I was stuck in post-concussion syndrome and wanted to write a book to help others who were experiencing a similar challenge. Surprising myself, I choked up when I spoke. My emotions were quite raw.

The other participants were experienced writers. One was a National Geographic photographer who used words that I had never encountered before. Deb and I were so out of our league! We were like Lucy and Ethel in the midst of serious writers. I hadn't known there would be professionals here! I wanted to pack up our things and leave then and there. I felt like a phony. A writer-want-to-be. Another participant was a woman who was paralyzed from the waist down due to a childhood accident with a tree. She shared her experience so gracefully and eloquently. Yet another participant had recently been diagnosed with Parkinson's Disease. Both were struggling with health issues far more serious than mine, and both had such upbeat attitudes. They seemed at peace, not bitter at all. Who was I to be writing about something as simple as being stuck in concussion recovery? Despite my trepidation, we were welcomed into the fold. The leader and all the participants seemed to embrace us and the minor-league writings we shared. No one in the group was pretentious. Everyone was down-to-earth, welcoming, and willing to build a safe space in which to write and share.

One of the first exercises Elizabeth gave us was to think of our "grand question." My mind flip-flopped between my head recovery experience and my retirement experience. Which was I writing about? Both felt like losses. One was a loss of my former self, and I still missed her. The other was a loss of my career. More than a job, it was my purpose. It was how I contributed to this life. It was how I tried to make the world a better place. So my grand questions that I recorded in my journal were:

"What do I do now?"

"How do I make a difference now?"

"Who am I now?"

This was deep stuff, and I could see that this

retreat was going to be therapeutic not just for my brain but also for my soul.

My plan to relax in the woods during our free writing time backfired. Our facilitator warned us that we would be asked to share a bit of our writing each time we reconvened. So I wrote. I was feeling sadder than I realized about my retirement, which then oozed into self-pity about my concussion. For our first round of free writing I wrote about my dad—another loss I was still grieving. My guilt about his nursing home experience bubbled up once more. I wrote about how I had thought the Universe was possibly punishing me with my head injury. How I wouldn't be free from my concussion until I had paid proper penance. I still knew on an intellectual level that this was absolute nonsense, but the feeling still returned, particularly when I was sad. I chose not to share this bit of writing during our group time because I knew I would not be able to do so without crying my eyes out.

Feeling pressure to write something that would be worthy of sharing with this all-star group of writers, I stepped outside our cabin-style room and sat down near a group of bird feeders. Several hummingbirds were vying for the sweet nectar in the feeders. They inspired me to write the following paragraph, which I shared with the group:

Watching the hummingbirds flit and flutter about in a frenzy reminded me of me. Of who I was before my head injury. I was a high-energy flitterer. I spoke quickly, walked fast, had no time for anything. Ironically, just weeks before I hit my head, I was sitting around a conference table with my leadership team. We had decided to share personal goals for the new school year, with a focus on our leadership styles. I shared, unnecessarily, that I tended to do things too quickly—think, talk, walk, even listen. My staff looked at me with knowing eyes as if my revelation was no surprise to them. My nickname at school was "Flash." I was known for speeding around the building in my suits and running shoes. So I confessed to my team of instructional leaders that I realized buzzing about the building at full throttle all the time wasn't necessarily a good thing. My goal for the year was to slow down. Walk and talk a little slower. Listen more deeply. The Universe has a strange sense of humor.

When I shared this excerpt from my journal, the group smiled and even laughed. They loved the part where I described being nicknamed

"Flash." And I loved getting an emotional response from my audience. In that moment I realized that I might be able to write this book after all.

Our facilitator, Elizabeth, had some advice that she used often: "Stay open to the tears and surprises. No tears for the writer, no tears for the reader. No surprises for the writer, no surprises for the reader." Powerful advice! She also led us in several short exercises that were equally effective and powerful. At one point she asked us to choose one image from our stories and have a conversation with it. My first reaction was skepticism, but I dutifully went to my corner of the room and began writing in my journal.

I chose to have a conversation with the cabinet door that I had hit my head on, causing my concussion. As I wrote out our conversation, I was both surprised and moved to tears. Here is what I wrote:

1957 Cabinet Door

Me: Why does your age matter?

Door: Maybe because you wouldn't have had the injury if I were a young cabinet door that stayed shut.

Me: Are you a metaphor for my own aging body and brain?

Door: Only if you want me to be.

Me: Why didn't you just stay shut?

Door: Because then you wouldn't have gone on the journey.

Me: What do you think I should learn from the journey?

Door: Stop fighting it.

Me: Easier said than done.

Door: That's what I thought when you asked me to just stay shut.

Me: That's interesting. What other words of wisdom do you have for me?

Door: I'm just a simple cabinet door that changed the trajectory of your life forever.

Me: You make it sound like a good thing.

Door: It is.

Where did that conversation come from? It took place in the course of a ten-minute writing exercise. Was my Inner Voice that had fallen mostly silent during my concussion finally waking up?

After writing my conversation with the cabinet door, I chose not to share it with the group. I knew my emotional runaway train was fired up and ready to go and once I released it, I would not be able to stop crying.

My sister and I enjoyed the Christine Center experience. It was not a luxurious spa, but it was a wonderfully soft place to land as we adjusted our sails for retirement. We hugged goodbye knowing we would be seeing each other again in just a few weeks. Malala Yousafzai was coming to Omaha for the annual Girls Inc. luncheon/fundraiser and I had purchased tickets for a table. Deb and her daughter were coming to Omaha for the event.

Back in April I had purchased the book *I Am Malala* for two of my female fourth-grade students who participated in Girls Inc. They both were bright, insightful girls who had dealt with their share of life's obstacles. Their mothers each gave permission for the girls to attend the luncheon with me. A few staff members, my daughter, and my husband sat at our table as well. It was a powerful experience. Malala herself is an inspiring speaker, and her story is very moving. But before she spoke, a local Girls Inc. teen and former Indian Hill student shared a poem. She was wearing her hijab as she shared her poem entitled "Dear Terrorist." Her words and her delivery stole the show! And as principal of Indian Hill, I could not have been prouder.

After the program we gathered around our poet and took pictures with her. Then one of my guest students announced that she needed to use the restroom. We followed her out into the hallway to help her find a bathroom with a short line. At this point, my head pressure was rising because there were a lot of sounds to filter out in the convention hall. I was also feeling my fatigue set in from all the excitement. The restrooms on the main floor all had very long lines, so we decided to try the second floor. We discussed using the elevator, then decided we could handle just one flight of stairs. The student let us know her situation was becoming urgent, so we climbed the stairs quickly. About halfway up the stairs, my sandal got caught in my pant leg and I tripped. I caught myself with my hands and didn't really fall all the way, but it was a jolt. My sister asked if I was all right, and I replied that I was just fine. But I felt it. That feeling again. My brain had been slapped up against my skull in just that little stumble.

After everyone was finished in the restroom we headed for the parking lot to get the car. As we approached the walkway to cross the street I knew I probably should not drive. I felt my response time slow down and the cloud set in. I handed the key fob to my sister. She drove the two students home,

I hugged them good-bye, and then we returned to my house. I promptly went to my room and lay down on the bed. I couldn't believe that this little stumble, where I didn't even fall all the way, could have caused me to reconcuss. What was going on?

My daughter, sister, and niece all gave me a big group hug as I let the tears of frustration flow. I was sick and tired of doing this dance. I went back to bed, knowing I would need to remain still for a few days. Walter Payton, my ever-faithful companion, curled up next to me. He would not move unless I did. He seemed to know I needed his company and comfort.

I stayed in bed for two full days and then slowly began moving about again. I had not experienced nausea with my first concussion, but with this one I felt nauseated if I stood for more than five minutes. The fogginess in my head seemed thicker than usual this time, too. At one point I was sitting on the couch and I said to my niece that I was really thirsty and needed to get up and get a glass of water. She looked stunned when I said it. When I looked to my right I saw that I already had a glass of water sitting next to me. I had absolutely no memory of getting it a few minutes earlier. I made an appointment with my doctor. I could not understand why I was seemingly reconcussing at the drop of a hat, and my short-term memory loss was freaking me out.

My doctor examined my eyes and found evidence that I had undergone some sort of trauma again. When she asked me to move my eyes up and to the side, it was difficult to follow her finger. I knew the eye exercises that I needed to do, and I assured her I would faithfully return to them. I also told my doctor that my anxiety levels were rising with this latest setback. My doctor thought I should try taking a low dose of Prozac, which might make me feel better and help me focus on healing. I also discussed my memory concerns and she recommended that I work with a speech therapist for a few weeks on specific memory exercises.

My first session with the speech therapist began with a quick assessment. After the assessment she looked a little surprised and said that I was testing in the normal range for my age. (I hated hearing that phrase "for my age"!) I told her that I was not able to remember anything if I was multi-tasking in any way. So she played some soft music and re-assessed. She immediately saw what I was talking about. I couldn't focus enough to remember when there was music, background noise, or conversation going on while I was performing a task.

After three short weeks of speech therapy, I had improved significantly. My therapist gave me a list of exercises and games to continue doing at home to maintain the progress I had made. One was a card game called "Two Back." Another person flips one card at a time and sets it down and I would have to name the card that was no longer showing. When we first started therapy I could only get through about half the deck before losing concentration, but now I could usually get through an entire deck successfully.

The speech therapist also had me download two free smartphone apps for improving focus and concentration. One was called "Mind Games" and the other was "Brain Trainer." I used these apps, along with my eye exercises, to start each day of my new life as a retired person.

I tried taking the Prozac my doctor had prescribed for me, but I felt as though it increased my anxiety. It may have been psychological, or maybe a concussed brain responds differently to these types of medication. Whatever the case, Prozac was not for me! I was anxious, which is very common with concussions. I was also feeling mildly depressed for a number of reasons. I was certainly grieving the loss of my career. I knew I needed to focus all my energy on healing, but

I felt guilty that I wasn't doing something to contribute to society. I couldn't help but feel a little like a quitter. The transition into retirement was emotionally very difficult for me. In addition, my stamina for keeping a stiff upper lip was eroding as I seemed to get knocked back down the rabbit hole every time I started to see daylight.

Like a lot of downtrodden people, I turned to prayer. I began each morning with some light yoga stretches. Then I would read from one of my two favorite books, *The Tao of Inner Peace* by Diane Dreher and *The Buddhist Path to Simplicity* by Christina Feldman. I had relied on both of these books for years during my morning quiet time before busy workdays. Their words of wisdom always brought me back to center. I would read short passages from each book and then meditate. After asking God for the strength to do what I needed to do to get through each day, I would then let my mind go blank, completely dark. This was a skill I was now accustomed to using, and I found it very soothing. I would sit for about ten minutes or so in nothingness. Beginning my days in this way kept me tethered to the hope that I would recover. This routine kept me from getting lost at sea.

12

Where Are You, Darlin'?

Nearly two years into concussion recovery, I was still grasping for ways to cope. I was also looking for the lessons I was supposed to learn from it all. I believe that the Universe teaches us important lessons if we are open to them. And when we haven't learned them to its satisfaction, then the Universe will sometimes repeat the lessons until we get it. Since I was surely getting repeated lessons with my head injury, I felt I had not yet unlocked the mystery of the lessons to be learned.

I had always been a spiritual person, although not a devout adherent of any faith. I had run the gamut of religious experiences. I was raised Missouri Synod Lutheran and attended Lutheran schools from kindergarten through high school. I became a "born again" Christian in college. Then

I became an "I don't know what the hell to believe anymore" agnostic after college. I became United Methodist as we raised our three children. I became Unitarian as Rick and I began our empty nest years. Through it all, I had always heard and listened to that still, small Voice deep inside me. Whether I called it Jesus Christ, God, The Universe, or simply Intuition didn't really matter. It had guided me throughout my life. But during the recovery from my head injury, my Inner Voice had been mostly silent. I tried to listen for it, but it was drowned out by the high-pitched buzzing in my brain.

Newly retired and able to focus on full recovery, I also began searching purposefully for my lost Inner Voice. I wrote the following entry in my journal just a few weeks after my fumble on the stairs at the Malala luncheon. Here is a glimpse into my mindset at that time:

> *A few days ago, while I was walking Walter in the woods, we came across a female deer. She was standing in the middle of the trail about 30 yards in front of us. She stood perfectly still and just stared at me. I stood perfectly still and just stared at her. She felt like a message from the Universe telling me that everything is going to be all right.*

I felt a quiet peace come over me—it was wonderful. The most hopeful I had felt in a very long time. I began to hear the whispers of my inner voice return.

Then tonight, again while walking Walter, I found a gorgeous, vibrantly blue feather. My six-year-old granddaughter loves bird feathers and collects them. The day before, we had found what we thought was a turkey feather. She and I Googled "turkey feather" together on my phone to confirm it was truly a wild turkey's feather. So, with my granddaughter in mind, I Googled "blue jay feather" because I was fairly certain that is what kind of feather it was. To my surprise, a website popped up explaining the shamanistic meaning of the blue jay feather (divinelotushealing.com). According to this website there are multiple meanings. I thought these two applied to me in that moment:

- *Choose a spiritual path and go as far down it as you can.*
- *If fear presents itself, attack it head on with courage.*

I'm not a believer in mystical truths, but I remembered the deer and now my blue jay feather. They felt like messages from the Universe, sent just for me. What was the message? Was the Universe reassuring me that I will get out of the rabbit hole after all? That is what it felt like, so I decided to believe it.

Even if believing in these signs of hope is mystical nonsense, I will believe it. Dumbo's feather allowed him to fly, not because the feather was magical, but because Dumbo believed it was. All I know is that believing the deer and the blue jay feather are signs of hope feels right; hope that I had lost. So I am grateful for the hope, wherever it comes from.

The still, small Voice deep inside me was getting a little easier to hear. I was able to connect to it again, and it felt wonderful. At this point in my healing process I began each day with a light, healthful breakfast followed by a plethora of vitamins and supplements. I would then scan the morning newspaper while enjoying a few cups of decaf coffee, giving my brain a chance to slowly warm up to the day. Next I would do my eye and brain exercises, which took about a half hour to complete. When I had done all that, I would do some light yoga stretching, then meditate and pray. I began with prayer first, then ended with silent meditation. I struggled at first with what to focus on and how to meditate. I hated focusing on my breathing, as is usually advised. Doing so made me feel as though I were hyperventilating. It raised my anxiety instead of decreasing it. So I searched for strategies that might work for me.

I had read somewhere about a person who began his meditation with "May I" statements, such as "May I bring joy to others today." I liked this strategy. It was simple and I could remember it. So I began my prayer/meditation time with three May I's before drifting into mental nothingness. I always began with "May I be healthy." I didn't want the Universe to forget how badly I wanted my full health back. The second two would change each day. At first I would just say two that sounded good off the top of my head, such as "May I be patient with my husband today." But that didn't feel genuine. After a week or so, I began to say my opening May I as "May I be healthy so I can serve." Then I would just be still and listen for my Inner Voice to tell me what to ask for. This became much more powerful, and whatever it was that came forward that day would often echo in my head at a later time, just when I needed the reminder. One morning I meditated on the words "May I have the strength of character to do what's right for my body today." But before I had completed the thought, the words "and forgive myself when I'm not perfect" popped up in my head. This was my Inner Voice reminding me not to be so hard on myself. Compassion for others begins with compassion for ourselves.

After my daily three May I's, I would sit completely still yoga-style and listen to the silence. It still felt very good to my brain when I practiced achieving this mental nothingness. My former self, the old me before the head injury, never would have been able to do this. I was too antsy and impatient to achieve this level of calm stillness. A head injury is a hell of a way to learn meditation, but it has certainly been one of the primary benefits of my concussion.

Beginning each day with these routines helped move my recovery forward. The eye and brain exercises helped me physically, and the prayer/meditation helped me remain hopeful. I was inching my way out of the rabbit hole. But as had happened all along the recovery route, I plateaued. I was five months into retirement but had not reached 100% yet. How could I get off this latest plateau?

In a lucky turn of events, I received a six-month free YMCA membership, along with free training sessions. I had participated in a year-long study for women with osteopenia, and at the conclusion of the year I could work with a trainer at the Y and learn specific exercises to strengthen my hip bones. Jill, the trainer who worked with me, was amazing. We began with a consultation to set goals. I warned her that I was still recovering from multiple concussions so I might be limited in what I could do. I explained that I might need to take brain breaks. She was very understanding and encouraging at the same time. She knew she could not push me or encourage me to push myself. To do so would have been counterproductive for a person with a brain injury.

I explained to her that I had something called "physiological post-concussion syndrome," which meant that my brain could not handle rigorous exercise yet. Further, I explained that elevating my heart rate would increase the pressure in my head. At this point I still could do only moderate exercise at best. Jill taught me a few specific exercises for my hips that mostly entailed squats with weights. I showed her how I took breaks between sets. I would sit down and put my hands over my eyes while using my thumbs to close my ears. Blocking out sight and sound was required to lower the head pressure and give my brain the recharge it needed to do another set.

I returned to the Y two days later to meet with Jill again. This time she had another trainer with her. She had explained my situation to a colleague who had worked with the University of Nebraska football team's trainers. He told me that he had worked with a football player who had symptoms just like mine. This particular football player had taken beta blockers to control his blood pressure, just like me. His brain pressure and pain increased whenever he tried to exercise, just like me. The trainer explained that the key to my getting back to rigorous workouts would be resetting my neurological system's response to exercise. That sounded good to me! He explained the importance of breathing and then proceeded to teach me a technique that concussed football players used. He had me lie on the floor and put my hand on my belly. I was instructed to take in a breath that raised my belly (belly breathing) for a count of 4, then slowly let the air out (count of 7), while holding my tongue to the roof of my mouth. It sounds a little strange, but it worked. It relaxed my skittish neurological system and my head pressure subsided.

After watching me do the breathing technique several times to ensure I was doing it correctly, the two trainers asked to meet with me to refine my exercise goals. They brought me into the trainers' office, shut the door to block out the noise of the weight room, and turned off the fluorescent lights. When they did these things without me asking them to, I knew I was working with people who understood the effects of concussion. We discussed my training goals as Jill took notes so I would remember what we had talked about. When we were done talking, I became very emotional and began to cry. These were happy tears. I thanked them both for being so understanding and told them that for the first time in two years I felt like I was being treated like an athlete with a head injury rather than an old lady whose "age is a factor." We had a plan in writing to get my life back. I felt so respected and understood. It was such a huge boost!

I continued to go to the Y to do my strength-training exercises twice a week. In between each set I would sit down, cover my eyes and ears, and do my belly breathing. I know I looked funny to the others in the weight room. Some concerned soul would invariably tap my shoulder and ask if I was okay. I would gleefully reply that I was great, just taking a little brain break! I think my reaction shocked them a bit, but it was hard for me to contain the joy I felt. I was moving off the plateau and exercising in ways I had not done in over two years.

Jill also had suggested that I try the weekly tai chi class that the Y offered, so I did. The class was absolutely life-changing. First of all, tai chi is slow-moving, quiet, and uses the vestibular system quite a bit. It's ideal for persons with head injuries. Secondly, having to follow the movements of the instructor while simultaneously listening to him was very challenging without being too challenging. It was exactly the amount of challenge that I needed. True tai chi is about moving your inner chi, or energy, around. I didn't care about the chi. I just knew that trying to follow the instructor and remember the 24 forms was good for my brain. I felt my stamina improving again.

I loved tai chi so much that once a week didn't seem often enough. I craved more. At this point in my recovery, I still couldn't remember the forms we were taught well enough to practice them on my own. I looked for classes I could take elsewhere to augment what I was learning at the Y. Our local community college held tai chi classes on

Saturday mornings. This instructor taught class very differently, but it was still enormously helpful and therapeutic. She taught parts of the form and had us practice the parts repeatedly. Just what I needed! "Part the Wild Horse's Mane" and "Wave Hands Like Clouds" were familiar to me, but now I could practice them in isolation repeatedly. This helped me remember better when we did the whole form on Wednesdays. In addition, my Saturday instructor devoted almost half the class to warm-up exercises before we began doing tai chi. The warm-up exercises were all brain-based and incredibly helpful. For example, she had us trace figure eights in the air, first with our right hand, then our left. At the first few classes, I couldn't do a figure eight with my left hand. But after repeated practice I could. I loved learning something new. I loved being physical. I loved feeling like my head was improving.

After months of these two tai chi classes, I discovered that our church also offered tai chi once a week. It was a different style, but I felt my brain was up to the challenge. Learning something new was healthy for recovery. This particular form was called Tai Chi Chih. I must admit that I was a skeptic about the whole "moving the chi" thing, but I do know my head felt great after tai chi class and I was moving off the plateau again.

Tai chi was excellent physical therapy. However, it was not aerobic in any way. I still needed to build my stamina by walking or running regularly. Winter had come once again, and I was not about to hijack my healing by falling on the ice again. I had no choice but to use the indoor exercise equipment at the Y. Walking on a treadmill is not the same as walking outside. Your feet land harder, so the impact is more jarring. It also uses a different kind of eye movement. My brain had to adjust to all this, but with time I was able to walk at a brisk pace for 30 minutes. I needed a brain break with belly breathing afterwards, but I could do it.

I was feeling the most hopeful and the strongest I had felt since my concussion. Another December came, and I was excited about the Christmas preparations. I loved, loved, loved baking holiday cookies. For the past two years I had been unable to do so without stressing my brain. I certainly wasn't able to bake and listen to Christmas music at the same time—one of my most favorite things to do. But 2016 was different. I could listen to the music, sing along loudly, and follow a recipe all at the same time. Huge progress! I told my daughter how excited I was to be able to sing and bake. She scurried off to find the Christmas present she had bought for me and asked me to open it early. It was the Pentatonix Christmas CD. I loved it! I played it over and over and over again, singing along off-key but happily. The joy I felt was indescribable. My caged spirit was finally being set free!

We rang in the new year with our closest friends, the way we had done before my concussion. Rick baked a wonderful meal of stuffed flounder, crab cakes, and fresh salad. We enjoyed the delicious lime cheesecake he had baked for dessert. I was able to stay awake until midnight, indulge in a little champagne, and talk for hours with friends without needing a brain break. I was sure that 2017 would be the year I finally made it completely out of the rabbit hole. I was feeling very hopeful, yet I would be reminded the following week that I wasn't out yet.

My oldest son and his wife had been given tickets to the championship college football game in Tampa, Florida. Tim was named "Nebraska Teacher of the Year" in 2016, and every state's teacher of the year was invited to the game for a special halftime ceremony honoring public school teachers. I had agreed to watch my granddaughters while Tim and his wife were away. I enjoyed my three-year-old and six-year-old granddaughters, but spending time with them was exhausting. Knowing this would be a challenge for me, my wonderful sister, Deb, planned to come to Omaha to stay with me and help with the girls. It was a week of waking to chatty little girls and talk, talk, talking all day. Walter and I had grown used to our quiet mornings and my routine of exercises and meditation. Not being able to center each morning and warm up slowly to the day quickly took its toll on my brain. About three days in, we were all sitting around the dinner table and Ellie, the three-year-old, started pitching a fit, as strong-willed three-year-olds sometimes do. I became overwhelmed with frustration. I ran into the bathroom, locked the door, shut the lights off and just sat in the dark with my ears covered. I felt like an autistic child who was on the verge of a meltdown and needed zero stimulation. Thankfully, my sister was there to take care of the girls while I sat in the dark regaining my composure. Incidents like this made me realize that even though I was doing much better, I still needed to remain mindful of my brain's needs and not ignore them.

We had an unseasonably warm end of January and February, so I was able to exercise with Walter outside on the Zorinsky Lake trail without worrying about ice or snow. This helped to improve my physical stamina as well as maintain my positivity. Here is an excerpt from my journal from January 30, 2017:

> *Was able to walk Walter a little over 4 miles for the second time in a week. My bladder gives out before my head. Hurray! I do feel pressure build, but if I focus on good breathing and keep walking, I do fine. As long as I take a break when I get home, I recover well. All I need is 2–5 minutes of sitting in silence and darkness, then I'm recharged and ready to go. I notice that I need a nap in the afternoon on days that I take the longer walks. It is cognitively tiring, but doable! Progress!*

It had taken two and a half years, but I was able to walk four miles without taking a break partway through. I had also started running a little. I called it gingerly jogging. In just a few months I was able to "run" most of my old two-mile route. I had come a long way since my geriatric five-minute walks around the cul-de-sacs in our neighborhood. I had made it this far by focusing on what I was able to do, not what I could not do. Dr. Jill Bolte Taylor talks about the importance of this strategy in her book *My Stroke of Insight*, which describes her own personal experience with a stroke and her eight-year road to recovery. Although strokes and concussions are not the same, they are both brain injuries and there are many similarities in regard to enduring the daunting recovery. The author emphasizes often the importance of remaining hopeful by focusing on what you are able to do, not on what you used to be able to do. I read her book twice and found it very inspirational, especially when I was struggling to remain hopeful.

As I read her book, I highlighted sentences that resonated with me, made notes in the margins, and used sticky notes to journal my thoughts. On page 159 the author writes, "This does not mean that I am in complete control of everything that happens to me. However, I am in control of how I choose to think and feel about those things. Even negative events can be perceived as valuable life lessons, if I am willing to step to the right and experience the situation with compassion." I underlined these words and then journaled the following on a sticky note:

> *Jill's comments about not wanting some of her old self restored and the ability to choose makes me think I've been hoping for the wrong thing. I shouldn't want my life*

back. I should move on and be better than before. Stop fighting it! Get out of the way of the change.

"Stop fighting it" had been a recurring theme throughout my healing process. I needed to remind myself of this often. When I surrendered to the situation, I would find calm and peace, and my head would feel better. But old, gritty, fighter me had a hard time letting go and just surrendering.

With the help of tai chi, daily meditation, and regular exercise, I was making progress and feeling my energy and stamina improve. But I hadn't reached 100% recovery yet. When I pushed too hard, I would still need to give my brain time to recover, although it recovered much more quickly now. I needed minutes or hours of recovery at most, not days. As pleased as I was that I had come this far, my goal was still 100% recovery and I was not there yet. I had contemplated acupuncture several times throughout this journey, and one day I saw a Facebook post with several recommendations for a local acupuncturist. The FB posts indicated that she was certified from "the best" school for acupuncture. She was also a registered nurse. I liked that she had knowledge of both Eastern and Western medicine, so I called for an appointment.

Maureen and I hit it off immediately. I felt like she was a great listener as I explained my frustration about my long concussion recovery journey. She said she could help. I told her bluntly that I was skeptical but willing to try anything. She responded to my skepticism by confidently telling me that it was perfectly fine, because I didn't have to believe in acupuncture in order for it to work. So we made a deal: I would remain skeptical and she would stick me with needles.

After only three sessions I noticed that my head felt lighter, clearer. The constant low-lying clouds in my mind lifted. One of my lingering symptoms had been not feeling the sensation of needing to urinate. I knew my bladder was full when my head pressure would increase. But after just a few sessions of acupuncture, I could tell when I needed to urinate without any increase in head pressure. Perhaps this sounds like a minor detail, but to me it meant getting one more piece of my life back.

In June I wanted to travel by myself to see my sister in Wisconsin for a few days. My husband offered to drive me, but I wanted to see if I could do it. I didn't quite trust my brain to handle the entire eight-hour drive in one day, so I made reservations at a bed and breakfast in Cedar Rapids, Iowa, so I could break the drive into two days. I was worried that driving across Iowa on Interstate 80 would be so dull that my brain wouldn't stay focused, so I planned a backroads trip. I brought my 35mm camera and stopped for impromptu photo shoots along the way. The trip to Wisconsin was wonderful! The drive was tiring, but in a normal way. I was actually able to listen to my favorite CDs and sing along while driving down the highway. It was so freeing! I enjoyed the independence as well as the beautiful Iowa countryside immensely.

The following month my son and his family were going to Wisconsin to visit my sister. Oconomowoc has lakes everywhere and is a wonderful escape from the uncomfortable heat and humidity of Nebraska summers. I wanted to join them, so with my newfound confidence in driving I decided to drive myself once again. But this time I made the trip in one day. It was tiring but in a normal way. I could do it! (I was careful to schedule my acupuncture treatment for just before the trip to optimize my chances of success.)

Then again in August I traveled to the coast of Maine with my husband and sister. We spent a week enjoying the cool ocean breezes on a part of the coast we had not explored before. As I walked through thick sand, ventured across sand bars, and climbed rocks on coastal islands I was in awe of what my brain could do compared with the year prior. I was feeling the shackles of PCS fall away.

When we returned home from our coastal trip, I was invited back to Indian Hill Elementary for the ribbon-cutting ceremony. A new school year was beginning, and the renovation of the school building had finally been completed. I was honored and very excited to be invited back for the ceremony. Afterward, I was given a tour of the newly remodeled building. Although the building had been fully renovated, the old cabinet door remained in place. As I walked into the classroom where my concussion journey had begun and glanced at that cabinet door, I was surprised that I had no emotional reaction. It was just a door.

As I continued to improve, I slowly began to return to my whirly-twirly old self. I was able to ride in the annual Corporate Cycle Challenge for the first time in three years. In the past I had ridden the 21-mile route. In 2017 I was only able to slowly ride the 10-mile route, but I remained focused on what I could do with the hope I would be able to ride 21 miles in 2018. My now eight-year-old granddaughter joined Rick and me for the Cycle Challenge, making it that much more special.

With all the summer travels and activities, I had departed from my routine. I hadn't done any tai chi in weeks. I hadn't been meditating or taking brain breaks either. I hadn't made an appointment for an acupuncture treatment since I was feeling so great.

I had returned to barging thoughtlessly through life again, and my symptoms began to return. First it was a dull headache with slight pressure and foggy thinking. Then I suddenly couldn't sleep at night again, which increased my symptoms.

I had thought I was out of the rabbit hole, but my head told me I wasn't. I am still learning to embrace a new way of life. In this new life, I have to be mindful, pay attention, meditate, and take breaks. My brain won't tolerate being pushed when it's tired, spinning thoughtlessly through the day. I can't lie to it about what it can and cannot do.

Old me still wants to flitter about, but buzzing about at full throttle all the time isn't really good for anyone. In late August I wanted to transplant some plants in my yard as well as plant some new bushes. I was anxious to complete this landscaping project and very much looking forward to it. But I was tired that day, and I could tell my brain just wasn't up to the physical task of such demanding labor. It was a little early in the season to transplant anyway. I decided it would be best to wait. Brain healing is a bit like gardening. You have to be patient and respect timing.

In the darkest days of my concussion, living one minute at a time was all I could handle. Learning to live in the moment was easy; a crash course, you might say. So as my brain heals and old me tries to revert back to my whirly-twirly ways, I remind myself to still those thoughts. Stay in the moment. Enter each moment with reverence. That familiar jukebox still turns on in my mind once in awhile. The song that plays now is an old Fleetwood Mac song called "Temporary One." The opening line is "Where are you, darlin'?" When my thoughts start twirling away from the moment, Stevie Nicks is there to sing me back. "Where are you, darlin'?" Oh yes, I am right here, wholly in this blessed moment.

Although my brain can now function at a fairly normal level again, it will not tolerate me barging mindlessly through life. What a gift!

13

Summary of Resources and Tips for Surviving the Rabbit Hole

I consider myself a strong person. Sensitive, but strong. When push comes to shove, I do what is necessary. I don't shy away from problems or difficult situations. Recovering from post-concussion syndrome has been unequivocally the most difficult challenge of my life. Being a strong person was barely enough to get me through. I was fortunate to have a talented and knowledgeable medical team as well as loving and supportive family and friends. Even with all these resources, staying resilient and hopeful often felt like an insurmountable challenge.

This final chapter summarizes in user-friendly form what worked for me. But as my doctor and concussion team often said, "When you've seen one concussion, you've seen one concussion." No two concussions are the same, but there are common strategies and resources we can use to facilitate the healing process. After listing strategies that were vital to my healing process, this chapter includes my call to action for both the medical and education industries.

Tips for Recovering from Concussion

Obtain quality medical care.

- Seek a physician who is certified in concussion care.
- Be an advocate for yourself. Speak up and ask questions. Take notes. (This can be very difficult for the person with a concussion, so parents, spouses, and support people might need to take on this role.)
- Could beta blockers help you? Check with your physician. I did not have high blood pressure by medical standards, but it was running high for me. A low-dose beta blocker was extremely helpful for managing the squeezing/pressure feeling in my brain.
- Should you take anti-inflammatory medications? I began taking these for

my arthritic back, but I noticed that they seemed to also lessen my head symptoms.

- Seek physical, occupational, and speech therapists who have experience working with people with head injuries.
- Explore alternative forms of medicine such as acupuncture.

Remember that resting the brain Is crucial.

- Sleep.
    - Honor your brain's need to sleep—don't fight it.
    - Establish a bedtime routine and use a sleep mantra if needed.
- Take brain breaks.
    - Be strategic—schedule the breaks. If you wait until you need them, you've waited too long.
    - The breaks need to be away from all visual and auditory stimuli. Finding that sweet spot of nothingness is balm for the broken brain.

- Meditate.
    - Read about meditation, and do what is comfortable for you.
    - Use a mantra or not, focus on breathing or not, pray or not. Experiment and find what works for you personally. Each person and each broken brain is unique.
- Take advantage of nature's healing qualities.
    - Walk in the woods.
    - Sit outside among the trees and birds.
    - Find ways to comfortably enjoy being outdoors in nature. It will help you maintain hope.
- Limit technology exposure (avoid brain drains such as TV, phone, computer, etc.).
    - This is a tough one, especially for teens with concussions. Parents must take control and limit their access to phones, computers, TVs. It is critical to the healing process. It's best to have no contact with technology at all at the beginning of healing from a concussion.

- Limit stress: Know what stresses your brain. Driving? Working full-time? Toxic relationships?
    - The concussed brain is already in a state of stress and anxiety. You must proactively seek ways to limit stress in your life to give your brain a chance to heal.
    - Keep your sense of humor! Find ways to laugh at yourself and the situation. (I became a hooker!)

Good nutrition is vital to the healing process because the brain's tissue has been damaged and needs to heal.

- No caffeine
- No alcohol
- Low sodium
- Minimize sugar
- Omega 3 fatty acids
- Lots of whole, natural foods
- Supplements (I found a lot of helpful information at healyourconcussion.com)
    - Fish oil! (24-3600 mg daily)

- ☐ CoQ10
- ☐ Turmeric
- ☐ High doses of Vitamin C
- ☐ Magnesium
- ☐ Bioplasma Cell Salts
- ☐ Melatonin: 1 to 3mg at night to help reset natural sleep patterns

Accommodate the injured brain.

- Get a good pair of noise-cancelling earbuds. These allowed me to endure meetings, stores, and even go to the theater and enjoy a movie. I also used them when traveling to drown out car or jet noise. Bose has the best for about $300. You can find cheaper versions online for about $40, but they are not quite as effective.
- Use a sleep mask to get complete darkness both for resting and sleeping. I used the mask in the beginning just to be able to be in my living room without pain. It also helped me sleep when I could achieve complete darkness. The mask is excellent for brain breaks!

- Take brain breaks BEFORE you need them. Schedule them. Find a quiet, dark space with minimal visual or auditory stimulation. I used a dark coat closet; it was life-saving!

Engage in safe levels of physical activity.

- Start with what you can do with minimal increase in symptoms. Using a scale of 1–10, don't go above a 2.
- Take brain breaks. Celebrate little victories. Be patient.
- Chunk it! If you can only walk 5 minutes, then walk 5 minutes, but do it two or three times a day. Break it down into little bits and slowly expand your exercise program.
- Yoga and tai chi: When you are ready, learn something new! Yoga and tai chi are excellent for the brain.

I had been avoiding yoga because I was afraid my brain would not like some of the challenging positions. I was very fortunate; however, that opportunities continued to come into my life just when I needed them. I had been following "LoveYourBrain.com" on Facebook. It provides resources and encouragement for people who have suffered from concussions and traumatic brain injuries. LoveYourBrain sent an email invitation for anyone who had suffered a concussion or any kind of traumatic brain injury (TBI) to participate in their six-week yoga class designed especially for people with head injuries. I signed up immediately and was grateful that Omaha had one of the few sites where the instructor had completed LoveYourBrain's special training course.

Once a week a small group of us with various degrees of TBIs met at Evolve to Harmony Yoga Studio where our instructors, Carol and Sarah, skillfully and compassionately led us through gentle yoga exercises, including breathing for relaxation. At the end of the hour, we always concluded with a 30-minute sharing time. We would gather in a circle, share our stories, and respond to weekly questions Carol posed for us. I found this entire experience to be both emotionally moving and rewarding. Until this experience, I had not realized how important community was. The circle sharing time became my favorite part of class and was immensely cathartic. The yoga was physically therapeutic, while the circle discussions were good for the soul. Connecting with others who have had similar brain injury struggles, yet found ways to remain positive, will boost your recovery process and help you remain positive.

Try doing brain exercises to improve your ocular motor skills, memory, and response time.

Note: Do these activities only when your physician says it is safe for you.

- Do daily crossword puzzles, word searches, Sudoko puzzles.
- Download and use free phone apps such as "Mind Games" and "Brain Trainer."
- Cook! Following a recipe while physically doing what it says (measure, pour, stir) is excellent for your brain.
- Read, read, read! Read for inspiration! If you can only read for a few minutes at a time, just read for a few minutes. Slowly rebuild your endurance.

Here are titles of books I found inspiring in some way:

The following books are not necessarily about head injury but are helpful in inspiring resilience:

- *The Book of Joy* by Dalai Lama, Desmond Tutu, Douglas Abrams

- *A Lucky Life Interrupted: A Memoir of Hope* by Tom Brokaw
- *Option B: Facing Adversity, Building Resilience, and Finding Joy* by Sheryl Sandberg
- *The Seven Spiritual Laws of Success: A Practical Guide to the Fulfillment of Your Dreams* by Deepak Chopra
- *Transitions: Making Sense of Life's Changes* by William Bridges
- *Wild* by Cheryl Strayed

The following books are specific to head injury:

- *A Stitch of Time* by Lauren Marks
- *My Stroke of Insight: A Brain Scientist's Personal Journey* by Dr. Jill Bolte Taylor
- *The Ghost in my Brain: How a Concussion Stole My Life and How the New Science of Brain Plasticity Helped Me Get it Back* by Dr. Clark Elliott
- *To Root and to Rise: Accepting Brain Injury* by Carole Starr

- *Coping with Concussion and Mild Traumatic Brain Injury: A Guide to Living with the Challenges Associated with Post-Concussion Syndrome and Brain Trauma* by Diane Roberts Stoler and Barbara Albers Hill

Practice acceptance.

Remember that accepting your head injury and current circumstance is not the same as giving up. You must surrender to the injury and slowly, patiently work on healing. But if you don't accept the injury and continue to try to live your life like you used to before your brain is ready, you will make your injury worse and it will take even longer to heal. Once post-concussion syndrome gets its grip on you, it is very difficult to escape.

Strive to remain hopeful.

- Surround yourself with optimistic people. Feel and accept their love and support.
- Focus on what you are able to do, not what you cannot do yet.
- Write in a daily gratitude journal. You will see that life does go on outside of your head injury.

- Read about others who have persevered. Find inspiration where you can.
- Get involved with an organization you care about (church/temple/mosque, book club, garden club, etc.). Do not become isolated!
- Join a support group for people with mTBI/TBIs. Connect to a community of survivors.
    - Loveyourbrain.com
    - www.pinkconcussions.com
    - Brain Injury Alliance (Most states have a state affiliate. In Nebraska it is the Brain Injury Alliance of Nebraska: biane.org)

A Call to Action: Research and Support Are Needed

- A recent study published in the *Journal of the American* Medical Association (JAMA) found that one in five teens report having had at least one concussion, and 5.5% have had more than one. We need to improve support for students with concussions in our schools. Nebraska has a "Return to Learn" law that requires schools to have defined protocols in place to support students returning to school after a concussion. It's a well-meaning law; however, it is yet another unfunded mandate for the education system. Currently schools and districts across the state are inconsistent in their implementation of the Return to Learn law.

- Educators need to collaborate with organizations such as the Brain Injury Alliance to define best practice protocols and support students with head injuries as they try to return to their school routines. Parents and students must be educated about the dangers of returning to a full work load too soon when after a concussion.

- In addition to supporting students, we also need to educate employers about concussions and recovery so that valuable employees do not lose their jobs as a result of their injury. This is especially true for those who sustain the injury while doing their job. For example, many of our first responders are inherently vulnerable to the dangers of concussion. We must support them when they have a head injury and help them find a way to use their skills safely while they heal.

- The medical industry, particularly emergency room doctors, need better education about recognizing the symptoms of concussion and educating the patient about the injury. Too many people have gone to an ER and been diagnosed with a concussion only to be told to go home and rest a few days. That is the only advice they are given. Very few doctors warn patients about the importance of taking concussions seriously and the dangers of post-concussion syndrome. Moreover, ER doctors often give the injured person verbal instructions. Relying exclusively on oral communication is not effective for a person with a concussion.

- Scientific research is needed regarding females and concussion recovery times. We already know from research that females concuss more often than males, and some research indicates that females take longer to recover. Currently the medical industry applies male concussion protocols to everyone, including females. Just as the medical industry learned that protocols and care for females who have suffered heart attacks differ from recommendations for males, I believe that with proper research we will also learn that female concussion patients need different protocols.

Final Words for People with PCS: Hold on to Hope

Maintaining a positive mindset is not easy for anyone suffering from a long-term health condition, but it is doubly difficult for the brain-injured person. Think about it. We must rely on our broken brains and broken hearts to get us through. A person's mindset is the most important factor in recovering from any type of head injury. You must find a way to remain hopeful, but not push yourself to do too much too soon. You absolutely must focus on what you are able to do, not what you cannot do yet. If that means being happy you can walk for two minutes before the exhaustion sets in, so be it. Celebrate the two minutes, because the two minutes will turn into twenty, and twenty will turn into forty. It may take a long time, possibly years, but it will happen. Hope is everything.

Epilogue

"Hope is not business as usual.
It is transformational. It is re-orienting
to a new star."

—Jan Phillips
(Hope Transforms.mov)

When I set out to write this book, my intention was simple and straightforward—to describe my physical recovery from a head injury. I expected that I would be completely symptom-free by the time I finished writing the book. That would be my happy ending. But as I chronicled what I experienced, I found myself realizing that more was happening than just my brain healing. My concussion journey was actually transforming me; my soul was healing. Hope has been the instrument that has allowed both healing and transformation to happen. As author and spiritual guru Jan Phillips writes, "Hope is the protector of potential."

My journey was more than just a physical healing. It was a shift in consciousness, a renewal of spirit. I allude to my spirituality throughout this book. I realize that the thoughts that I shared are sometimes contradictory. But that is part of my journey, too. Sometimes I get it— who God is and what that means in my life—and sometimes I don't.

When I retired from a career that I loved, I felt like I had lost my purpose. I temporarily lost my identity. If I wasn't the principal of Indian Hill Elementary any longer, then who was I? With my injured and altered brain, how could I make a difference now? After more than three years of concussion recovery, I have found an answer. My purpose in life is simply to be a force for good in this broken world—however and wherever I can help make things happen.

Recently I have been lending both my time and my story to the Brain Injury Alliance of Nebraska (BIA-NE). I have been working with the organization's executive director, Peggy Reisher, and we have been using my connections in the education world to bridge the gap between BIA-NE's resources and the places where these resources are needed in the school system. Peggy had been trying for four years to build that bridge with minimal success. But my concussion story and my experience as an educator seem to be opening doors for BIA-NE, and the right people are listening. We have met with members of the Nebraska Department of Education, members of the State Board of Education, and the executive directors of organizations that support both administrators and teachers. Our goal in these meetings has been to move everyone beyond just concussion awareness to full compliance with the state's Return to Learn Law. This law mandates that every school in Nebraska create a written policy that states specifically how the school will support and accommodate students with concussions when they return to the classroom. As of this writing, we are still in the process of working with these various organizations.

In response to one of these meetings, the executive director of the Nebraska Council for School Administrators, Dr. Mike Dulaney, decided to highlight the Return to Learn Law as the cover story in the association's monthly magazine. My personal concussion story will be included in the article to highlight the importance of proper concussion care and management in the school setting.

In addition to sharing my story with the education system of Nebraska, I have shared it with an organization called Love Your Brain. This organization was founded by Kevin Pearce and his family. Kevin was a snow boarder who sustained a serious traumatic brain injury while training for the 2010 Olympics. An award-winning documentary called "The Crash Reel" was produced to chronicle Kevin's experiences. Love Your Brain provides resources and information for brain-injured persons and their families. My story was featured in the Community Stories section of their website in November 2017. This section is specifically for sharing stories of resilience to offer hope and encouragement to anyone suffering from a brain injury. I feel humbled and honored that my concussion story is being used to improve the lives of others.

I plan to continue being an advocate for people with brain injuries. I now serve on the board of directors for the Brain Injury Alliance of Nebraska. I will continue to lend my story and my voice so that appropriate changes can be made in both the education and medical industries. In particular, I hope that my story will be a true call to action for medical professionals to evaluate and revise current concussion protocols. I predict that in the near future we will see that protocols for males will no longer be applied to females. Research will be done to provide better care for the vulnerable female brain, and fewer of us will become trapped in post-concussion syndrome.

In addition to doing brain injury advocacy work, I hope to become a certified tai chi instructor. I am not ready yet. I still need to learn more about the martial art and hone my skills before I can teach it. But I hope to teach it one day and share the benefits of tai chi with members of the brain-injured community.

Today I no longer need to take beta blockers or anti-inflammatory medications. (I still take a plethora of supplements, though.) I still get headaches on occasion and become fatigued if I am not mindful of my brain's needs. I still have minor memory and balance issues when I am very tired. I understand the dangers of getting another concussion, so I am hypervigilant to avoid bumping my head or falling. I am aware that I have an increased chance of dementia later in life due to my multiple concussions. Despite all this, I can honestly say I am the happiest I have ever been. I am acutely aware of the sweetness of each moment and each day. I am happy because I choose to be.

In the process of sharing my recovery story, I came to realize that everyone gets stuck in a rabbit hole of one kind or another. Grief, cancer, mental health issues, arthritis, and divorce are all examples of rabbit holes. Rabbit holes are dark and uncomfortable, but they can transform us if we let them. Post-concussion syndrome was my rabbit hole. What is yours? Whatever it is, my advice is twofold. First and most importantly, find ways to remain hopeful. And second, stop fighting the transformation that is taking place as a result of your experience.

Although my recovery journey has been daunting and very difficult, I have emerged from the rabbit hole a better, stronger person. Despite any lingering symptoms or worries, I love my life and who I am today. I have been transformed to a calmer, more content version of myself. I have stopped trying to return to business as usual—the Flash. I love the new me and am very optimistic about my future. I have re-oriented to a new star, and life couldn't be sweeter. I hope the path out of your own rabbit hole leads you to a similar place of peace and joy.

About the Author

Sharon Royers was an elementary school teacher and principal with the Omaha Public Schools for eighteen years before retiring due to a brain injury. She was also an adjunct instructor for the University of Nebraska at Omaha and Concordia University. She currently serves on the Board of Directors for the Brain Injury Alliance of Nebraska. Her concussion story has been shared by LoveYourBrain.com and the Nebraska Council of School Administrators. She continues to advocate for the brain injured by working to ensure all schools in Nebraska have the tools to comply with the Concussion Awareness Act and the Return To Learn Law.

Sharon is originally from the Chicago area but has lived in Omaha, Nebraska for the past twenty-two years with her beloved partner and husband, Rick Royers. Together they have raised three children and now enjoy time with their two granddaughters.

52766392R00138

Made in the USA
Columbia, SC
11 March 2019